33A-T-ASL

How to Write American Sign Language

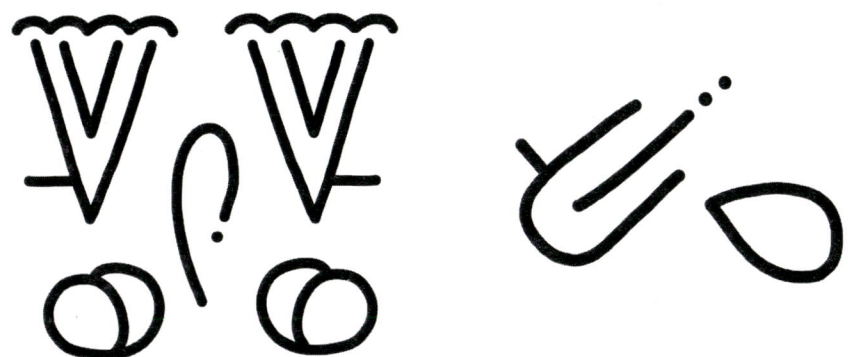

by Adrean Clark

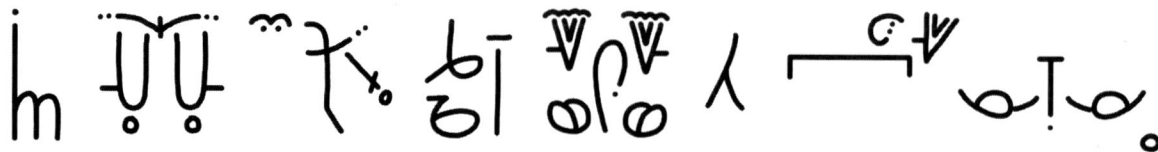

For all generations of signers. May the past be preserved and the future built.

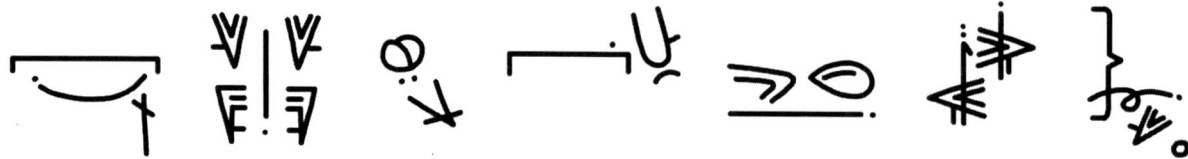

How to Write American Sign Language

Copyright © 2012 by Adrean Clark.
Published by ASLwrite in Burnsville, Minnesota.

Si5s concept by Robert Arnold.

Photographs by Julia Dameron and Erik Call.
Models (in order of appearance): Julia Dameron, Montrell White, and Amber Zion.

ISBN-13: 978-0-9858768-0-7

Library of Congress Control Number: 2012912030

All rights reserved. Without limiting the rights under copyright reserved above, no part of this publication may be reproduced, stored in or introduced into a retrieval system, or transmitted, in any form, or by any means (electronic, mechanical, photocopying, recording, or otherwise) without the prior written permission of both the copyright owner and the above publisher of this book.

Table of Contents

Acknowledgments 4

Introduction 5

Chapter One: The Digibet 6

Chapter Two: Diacritics 19

Chapter Three: Movement Marks 29

Chapter Four: Locatives 43

Chapter Five: Extramanual Marks 53

Chapter Six: Indicators 63

Chapter Seven: Composition 73

Resources 87

Answer Key 94

Acknowledgments

This book would not be possible without the vision of Robert Arnold (si5s.org). His hours spent tutoring me and our time working together on developing this amazing language are much appreciated. He also had valuable input on the contents of this book.

I could not have become fluent without the help of Julia Dameron (juliadameron.com), who was instrumental in creating the early American Sign Language Writing Dictionary. Our days writing pushed the boundaries of the written language.

There are also a few other people who contributed: Erik Call, Montrell White, Amber Zion (amberzion.com), Alison Aubrecht (facundoelement.com), and Raymond Luczak (raymondluczak.com). Erik took the digibet photographs, while Julia shot Montrell and Amber as the models for the Diacritics and Composition chapters. Alison and Raymond helped test this book, making sure the content was clear and accessible.

What you read in the forthcoming pages would not be as polished without the fantastic editing skills of John Lee Clark, who also happens to be my husband. Our sons remind me every day of the importance of the language of love, and for that I'll always be thankful.

Adrean Clark

Introduction

"If I cannot write in my own language, then who am I?"

Robert Arnold pondered this question one day as he wrote in English. A native Deaf signer, he felt incomplete in that he was borrowing another language to express his thoughts. This troubled him for years. Finally, in a coffee shop in New York City, a solution burst upon him as he doodled a few handshapes on paper. Those early digits were the beginning of a way to write in his native language, American Sign Language.

Robert is not the first to invent a method for writing ASL, but his is the first to provide a support for fluency. Si5s, named after the handshapes for the word "signing," is a full-fledged writing language that provides scaffolding for advanced concepts. It is to signed ASL what written English is to spoken English.

For us to understand what Si5s is, we must also understand what it is not. Previous attempts at writing in ASL fall into two groups. The first group tends to be direct illustration—drawn images of the face, body, arms, and other pictorial details. Si5s is not like that, because it uses only the lines and strokes necessary to convey each distinct sign.

The other group is made up of notational systems, which some linguists have used to record on paper signs, such as "Pro-1" representing the sign "me." Those systems tend to be complex and difficult to learn. Si5s is connected enough to signed ASL that you can read a ASL word on paper for a sign you have never seen before and be able to sign it right, in the same way an English speaker can pronounce a new word accurately without having heard it spoken before or reading a pronunciation guide in a dictionary.

To further understand the nature of written ASL (Si5s), study the following chart:

Signed ASL	Written ASL
Handshapes	Digits
Palm Orientation	Diacritics
Movement	Movement Marks
Spatial Orientation	Locatives
Nonmanual Signals	Extramanual Marks

The chapters in this book follow the same format, to allow for easier comprehension. An effort has been made to provide ideal content for both classroom and home study. If you are fluent in ASL, then half the work is already done! The rest is a matter of practice.

It is our dream that one day we will enter a library or a bookstore and find there stacks of books in written ASL. As we open those books, we are drawn in, connecting with the rich literary roots of our community and its language.

The author will be you.

Chapter One: The Digibet

American Sign Language is visual communication. Concepts are mostly conveyed through the hands, supported by the body and facial expressions. To learn written ASL, we need to know what consists the language. The five main components of ASL are handshapes, palm orientation, movement, spatial positioning, and extramanual signals (also known as nonmanual signals).

Of all five components, the most essential are the *handshapes*. Each handshape has its own meaning, and it is built upon to show a variety of concepts. In written ASL, handshapes are represented by *digits*.

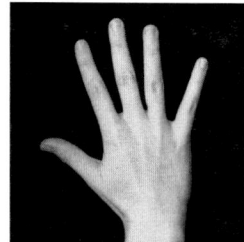 

Handshape   Digit

When we think of handshapes in ASL, we usually think of the manual alphabet.

The manual alphabet, while useful for fingerspelling terms and initialized signs, is not native to ASL and does not feature all of the handshapes that are used most often. What we will draw on instead is the *digibet*, or ⱽ⊘⊃.

Reading the Digibet

The word "digibet" comes from combining "digit" and "alphabet." It is easier to visualize a digit when you match the written digit with the actual handshape.

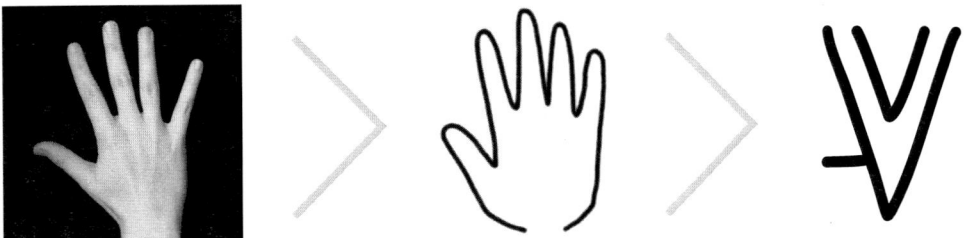

The next couple of pages have 30 of the most commonly used digits, which represent the building blocks of American Sign Language. They are also sequenced into the digibet. While used frequently, those digits do not encompass all of the possible handshapes that signers use. (The extended digibet is in the Resources section.)

As you study the digibet, watch the position of the thumb. This gives you important information on the direction the right and left hands are facing. The thumb location is also called the *chereme*, the smallest unit in writing that orientates the writer and reader.

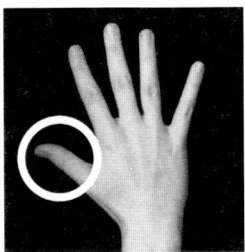 

Note that palm orientation is marked by the separation of the right/left hand digits. Other ways to show this orientation are covered in later chapters.

Left Hand | The American Sign Language Digibet

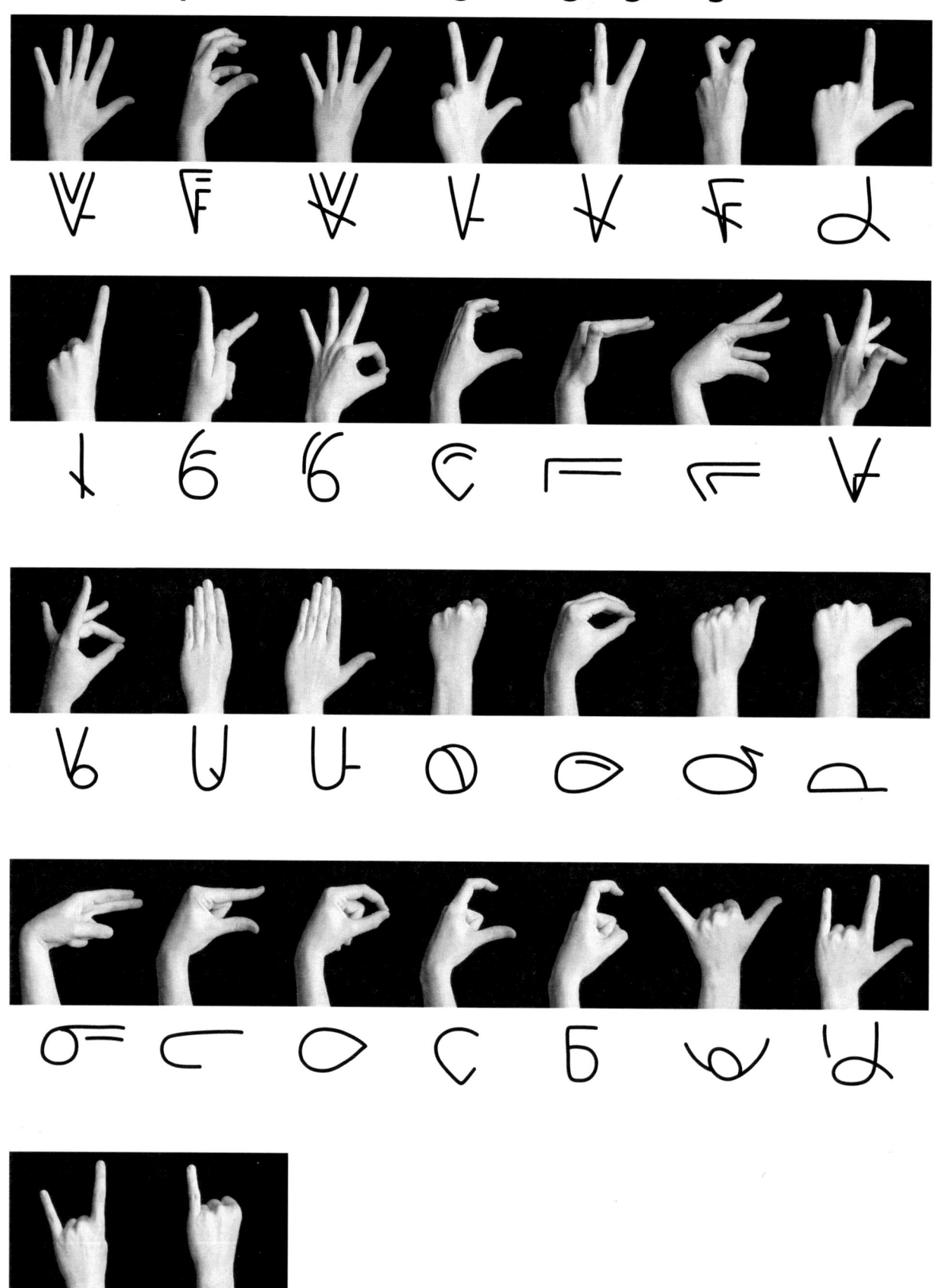

How to Write American Sign Language

The American Sign Language Digibet | Right Hand

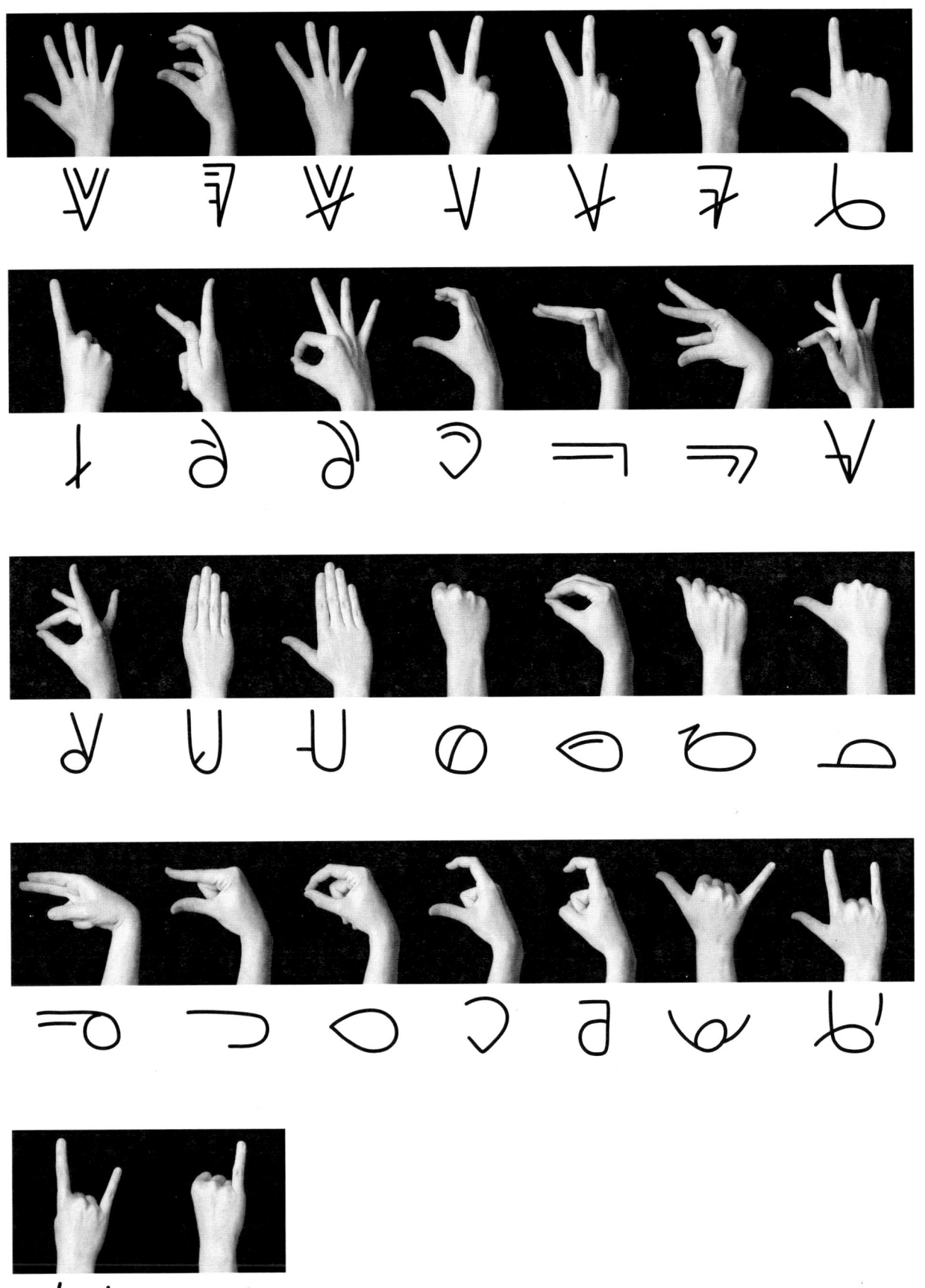

The signer's hand dominance is also revealed by the cheremes. If you tend to sign using your right hand, that is your dominant hand. You would use the right-hand digibet more, especially when fingerspelling words. This is a unique feature of written ASL, allowing readers to identify left- or right-handed signers by their writing.

Writing Digits

The digibet may look foreign at first, but as you take time to read and write them, the patterns behind the handshapes will become clear. They are split into three categories, and each category is named by the first handshape in the extended digibet sequence:

Open Digits (𝒲): Handshapes that mainly have the fingers in an extended position.

Closed Digits (𝒪): Handshapes where the fingers and thumb are touching each other in a mostly inward position.

Mixed Digits (⌐): Handshapes that have both extended fingers and touching fingers. They aren't quite open or closed, but a combination of both.

The listed digits together create the name sign for the digibet, 𝒲𝒪⌐. By looking at the basic shape of the handshapes we can also understand how exactly the digits are written. Always start writing using the larger line first. You may also trace the digit examples with your index finger to become familiar with the shape and stroke order.

The chereme also tips us off on which direction to start writing the digit. If the thumb sticks outward, then the following patterns emerge:

Once the thumb makes contact with the index and other fingers, lines cross over each other:

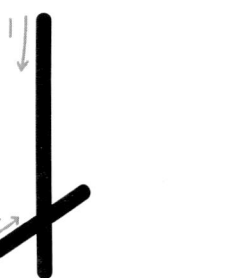 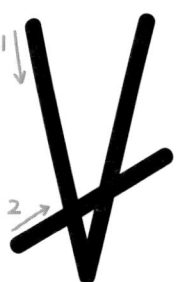

A quarter-view also emerges in some handshapes:

Sometimes the thumb disappears altogether, leaving the shape of the palm and fingers. When this happens, the little finger takes on the role of the chereme:

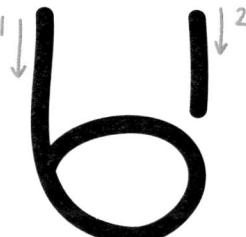 

A digit may also be related to another digit. Can you see how in the following example?

 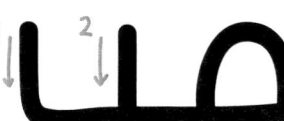

Another way to become familiar with the digibet is by memorizing the manual alphabet. Here it is again, in left-handed and right-handed versions.

Left-Handed Manual Alphabet

Right-Handed Manual Alphabet

Laurent (left-handed)   Laurent (right-handed)

It might feel odd to write the digits when you start, but it helps to visualize the handshapes and the digits together in your mind as you write. Over time it will become an automatic process.

In the next chapter, we will add motion to digits through movement marks.

Exercises:

Match the handshapes to the digits:

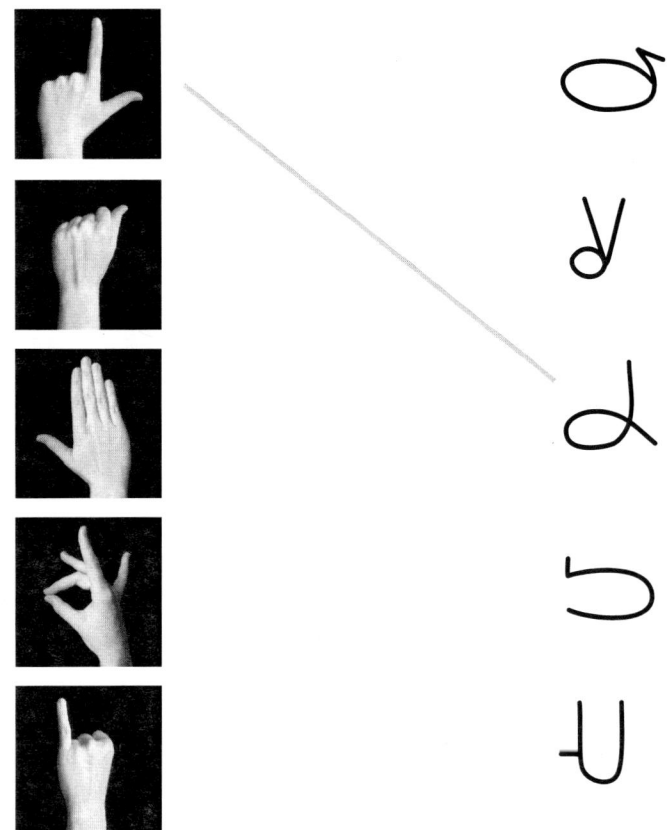

What names are spelled out below? Is the writer left- or right-handed?

☐ 6 ⌿ ◯ ⋎ 6: ___EDWARD (LEFT-HANDED)___

⌸ ⌶ C ⌿ ◯: _____

⌒⌸◯∥ ∥⌿◯◯◯C⌸⌶: _____

◯C◯⌿◯⌿◯ ⌿◯⌿◯⋎◯⋎: _____

⌿ ◯C⌿⌿⌿⋎⌸⋎ ⌿◯⋎C: _____

How to Write American Sign Language

Practice:

Chapter Two: Diacritics

In ASL, handshapes are not static. We shake our handshapes, flip our wrists back and forth, and swivel our hands into circles. In written ASL, the symbols that show those motions are called *diacritic markers*, or *diacritics* for short.

The five diacritics are the hinge, rotational, flutter, rattle, and edge diacritics.

Hinge   Rotational   Flutter   Rattle   Edge

Hinge Diacritic

When the wrist moves in a back-and-forth motion, an arc is used to represent it. The *hinge diacritic* can be either a back-to-forth or side-to-side motion. The specific motion depends on context.

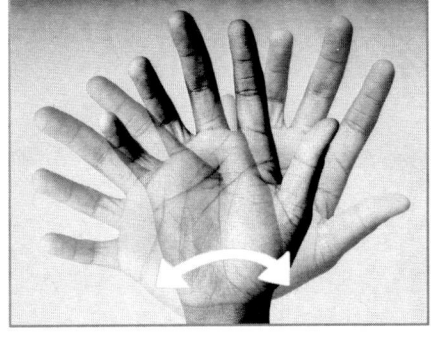  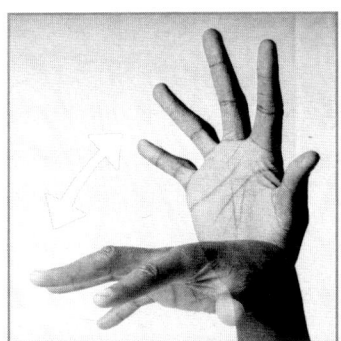

How to Write American Sign Language   **19**

Take the sign "yes" for example. When moved once, the arc of the hinge diacritic is enough. When the handshape is moved at least twice, dots appear under the arc as a counter. (Most nouns require a counter, while verbs usually have a single motion.)

Yes   Yes (2 times)

Rotational Diacritic

The *rotational diacritic* uses a circle symbol. A secret to identifying the difference between back-and-forth motion and rotational motion is feel the bones of the forearm. If the bones move past each other when you sign, then the rotational diacritic is written.

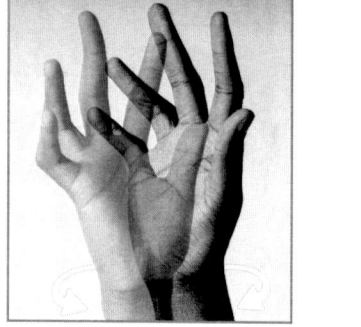

"Finish" demonstrates the usage of this diacritic. Again, a counter can be used below the circle.

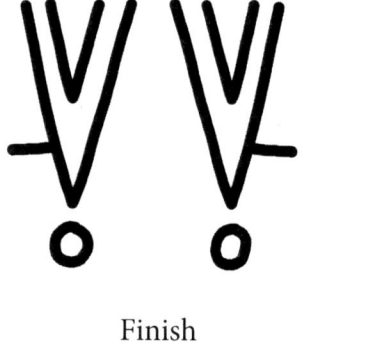
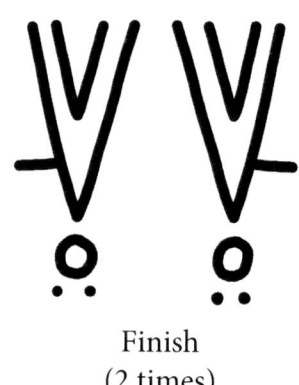

Finish   Finish
                  (2 times)

How to Write American Sign Language

Flutter Diacritic

The effect of wiggling our fingers is made through the *flutter diacritic*.

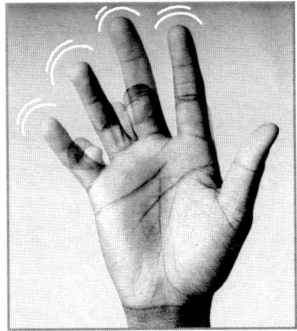

It tends to go with the open-handed  digits. In this example, the word "wait" is used.

Wait

Rattle Diacritic

The shaking of a handshape is often used with name signs. The motion is not large enough to warrant the side-to-side representation of the hinge diacritic, but still noticeable. For this movement, the *rattle diacritic* comes in.

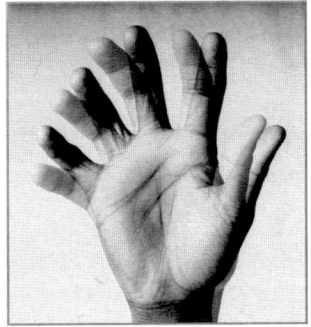 

Line placement is important, as it marks whether a single finger or the entire handshape moves.

Democrat   Questioning ("Is that so?")   Dog

Edge Diacritic

The edge diacritic, while not actually a movement, helps establish the handshapes in neutral space. It shows whether the handshape is held in its default view or set on end.

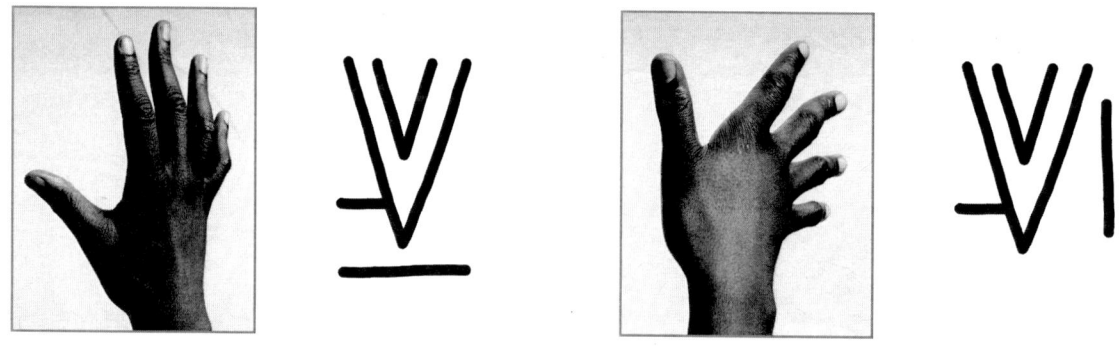

Compare the three digits below. The first digit means "three." Adding the edge diacritic turns it into a car parked on the street, and finally, a car that's landed onto its back bumper.

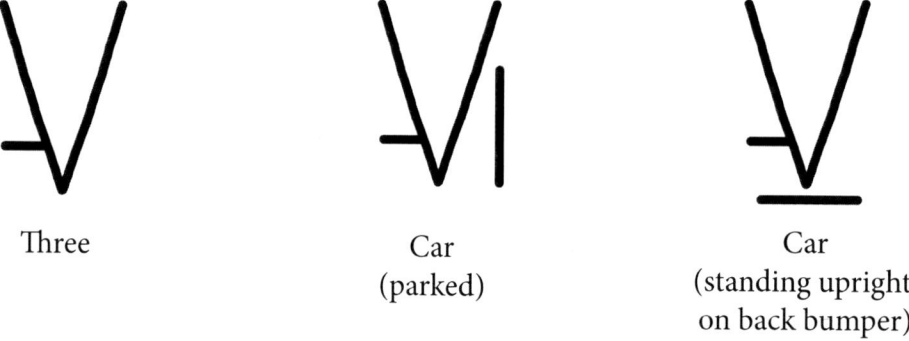

Three   Car (parked)   Car (standing upright, on back bumper)

A slight change in the diacritics can transform the meaning of a digit. For example, by using double curve lines, you can change a straightforward "finish" to a grumpy "that's enough."

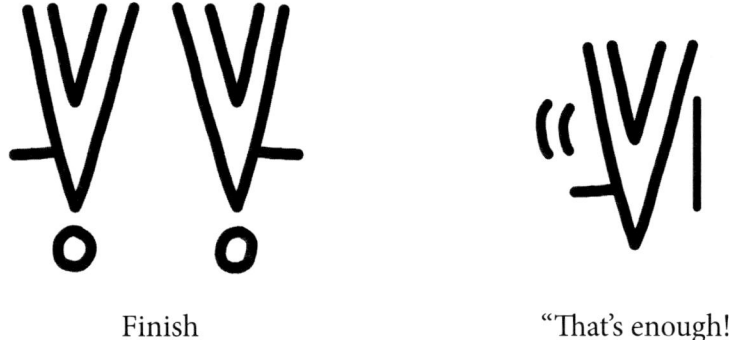

Finish   "That's enough!"

The five diacritics are essential for writing wrist motion and handshape movement. Finding the right one is important for accurate writing. In the next chapter, we will cover larger movements.

Exercises:

Circle the diacritics that fit the handshapes in the following words:

Apple	⌒	Ⓞ	〜〜	))	—
Snow	⌒	○	〜〜	))	—
Must	⌒	○	〜〜	))	—
Dog	⌒	○	〜〜	))	—
Machine	⌒	○	〜〜	))	—

Write the diacritics that support the digits in the following words:

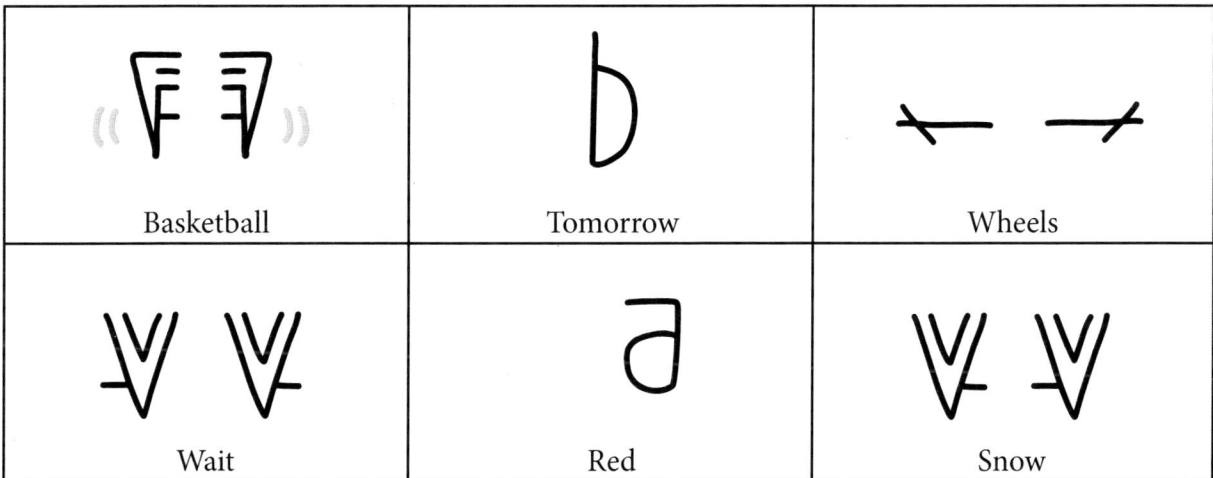

| Basketball | Tomorrow | Wheels |
| Wait | Red | Snow |

How to Write American Sign Language

Practice:

Chapter Three: Movement Marks

The spatial area we have explored in writing so far is the airspace directly in front of the upper torso. This location is called *neutral space*. The movement marks are directional signals that help you visualize how the signs move in that space. There are three groups of movement marks: Motion lines, endpoints, and steering marks.

Motion Lines

When writing in ASL, the first-person perspective is the default perspective. If we attached a pen to your dominant hand, you'd see a trail moving in accordance with your hand while you sign. On paper, this "trail" is the *motion line*. If your hand goes right, the digit on paper goes right.

An *endpoint* "finishes" the motion line, informing the reader which direction the digit moves in. It can also add tone to the motion. We will cover that shortly.

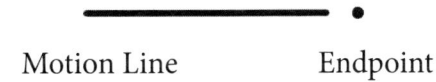

Motion Line   Endpoint

Motion lines have two functions, directional and conceptual. The *directional function* directly represents the route of movement for the digit. The three basic types of directional motion lines are straight, patterned, or random.

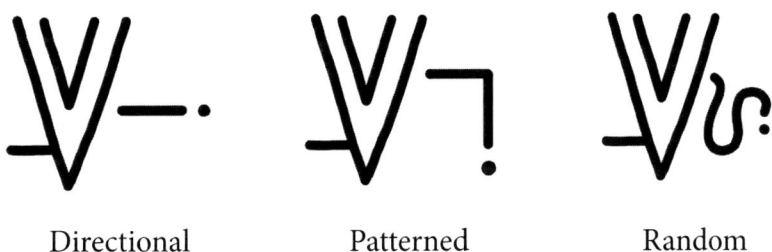

Directional   Patterned   Random

How to Write American Sign Language

Directional motion lines are the most common form. When in neutral space, the motion lines follow the horizontal motion of the sign as it moves closer and further away from the body. When signs move up and down, instead of forward and backward, the *vertical mark* is added.

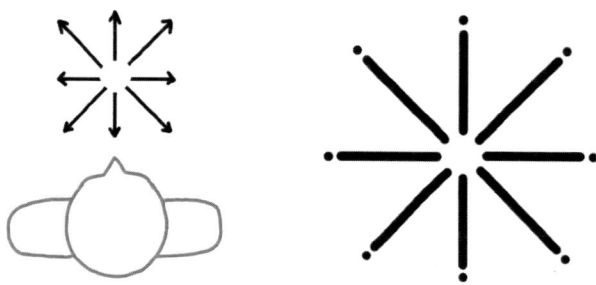

Neutral Space - Horizontal

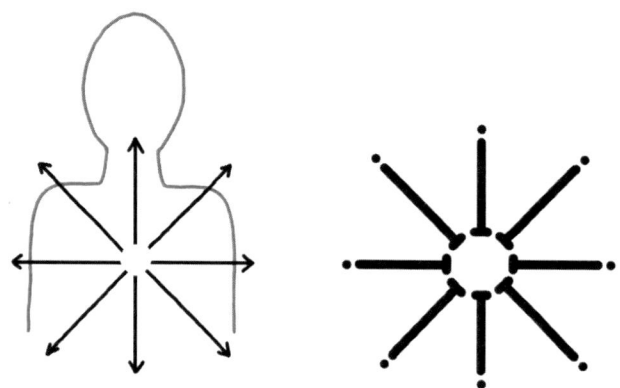

Neutral Space - Vertical

Look carefully at the following words to see how directional motion lines work.

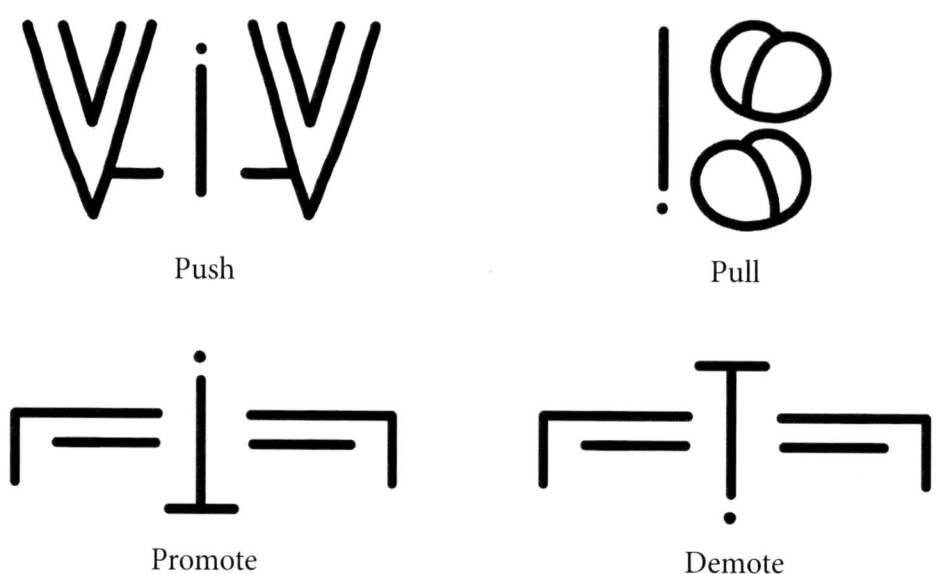

Push　　　　　　　　　　　　　　Pull

Promote　　　　　　　　　　　　Demote

Patterned motion lines follow a consistent route. A classic example is the horizontal then downward movement for certain city names.

Austin   Indianapolis

Zigzags and circular lines fall under this category as well. One example is the zigzag of the sign "here." Other signs also follow this pattern.

Here   Winter

Random motion lines are creative. They don't follow a set pattern. For example, a story about a car in a wild chase down a street could have random motion lines to help fill in the picture.

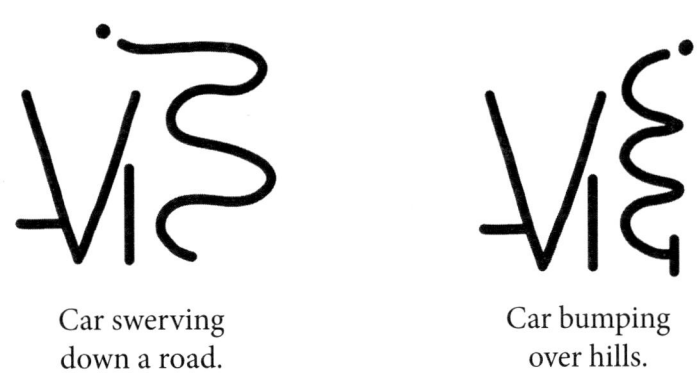

Car swerving down a road.   Car bumping over hills.

Directional motion lines can be combined, as in writing "give to three people."

Give to three people.

How to Write American Sign Language

Motion lines behave a little differently when it comes to digits that move alternately and away/toward each other. Specific marks are useful for those situations.

The *alternating mark* identifies which handshape moves first in a word. It always faces inward. There must be at least two endpoints above the alternating mark to show that the motion returns to the first digit.

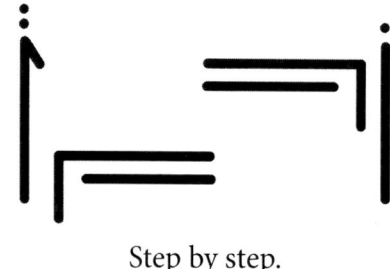

Step by step.

When the handshapes touch each other then move away, the *expanding mark* notes the point of contact. It resembles the vertical mark but does not signify vertical motion. "Sentence" is a good example.

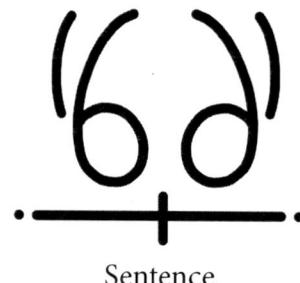

Sentence

If the action is in reverse, the *contraction mark* appears between the motion lines. It is actually an endpoint, but the key thing is how the endpoint is used.

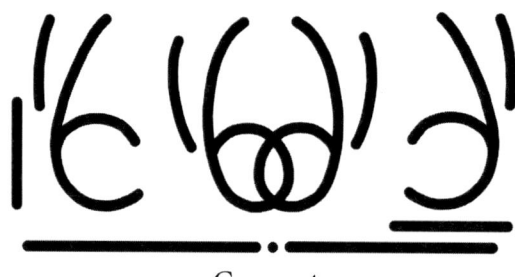

Connect

The vertical mark also has two variants, convex and concave. For a combination of vertical and horizontal movement, use the concave and convex vertical marks. To describe the motion of a kid sliding down a waterslide, you would use the *concave vertical mark* as follows:

A description of a traveler roving over hill and dale would fit best using the *convex vertical mark*:

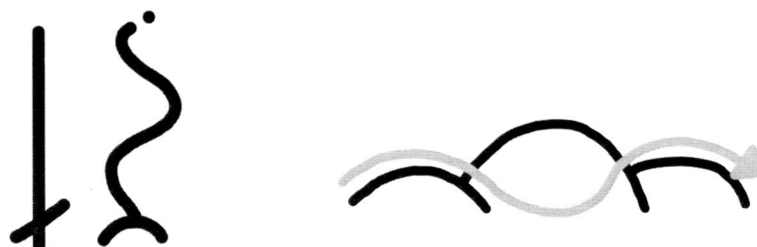

The second function of motion lines is the *conceptual function*. It still shows motion, but is more about time and space rather than straightforward movement. This is done through morphing and instance lines.

A *morphing line* is a motion line that identifies when a handshape represented by a digit changes, or morphs. The actual movement of the sign does not necessarily follow the motion line.

And

When it does become important to clarify that the morphing sign doesn't move in space, the *static mark* "nails" the digits into place.

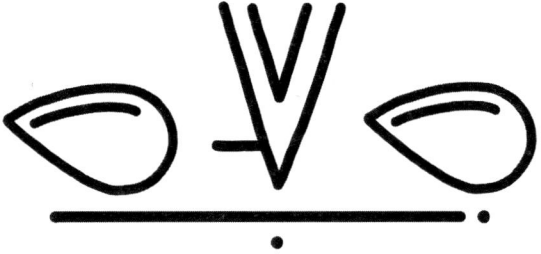
Taking A Picture

The *instance line* creates a temporal delay between the repeating motion of a sign, such as in the word "happen."

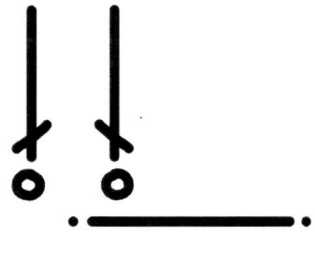
Happen (Twice)

How to Write American Sign Language

In using motion lines with digits it's essential to remember that the handshape that is used at the beginning of the sign is the one that is documented. If the handshape changes in transit, then the beginning and ending digits are written.

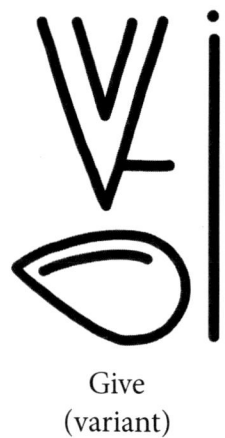

Give
(variant)

Endpoints

As previously shown, the dot at the end of a motion line is called the endpoint. They mark the amount of times a movement takes place. In ASL structure, the endpoints also indicate nouns and verbs. More than three endpoints are usually not necessary.

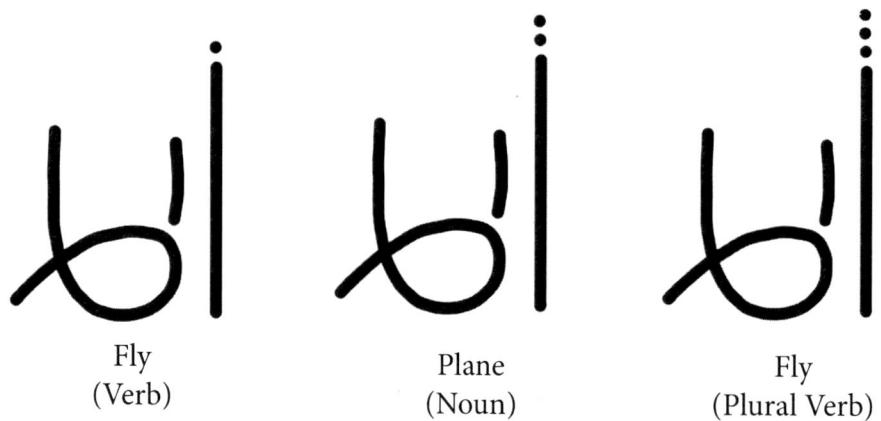

Fly
(Verb)

Plane
(Noun)

Fly
(Plural Verb)

Endpoints also change with emphasis. *Firmpoints* are the equivalent of exclamation marks in English.

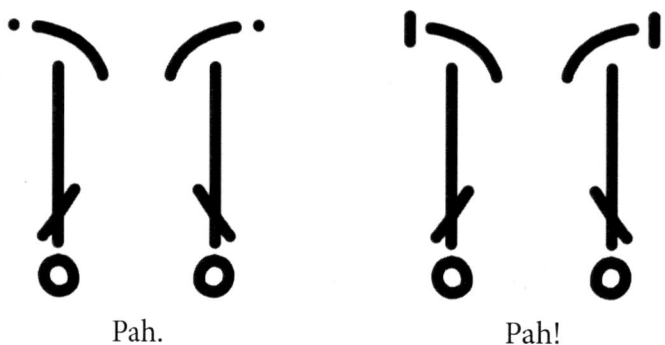

Pah.

Pah!

A *contact point* is an endpoint without motion lines. This shows where a handshape touches the body, the other hand, or an imaginary surface in the air. If a two-handed sign contacts in neutral space, the dominant hand is almost always written on top.

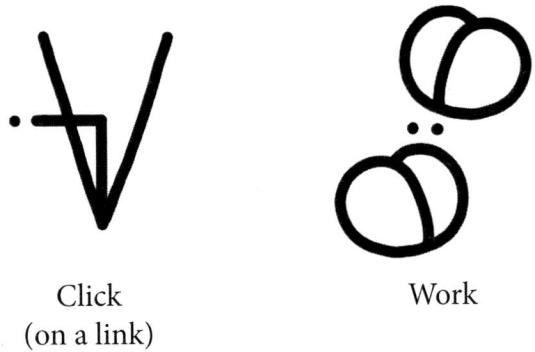

Click
(on a link)

Work

Steering Marks

When signs rotate around each other, the *steering mark* is used. It resembles the circle diacritic but is placed in the center of the orbiting handshapes. The two directions are vertical and horizontal.

The *full steering mark* can mean that the handshapes rotate over/under, like the word, "year," or past each other, as in the word "change."

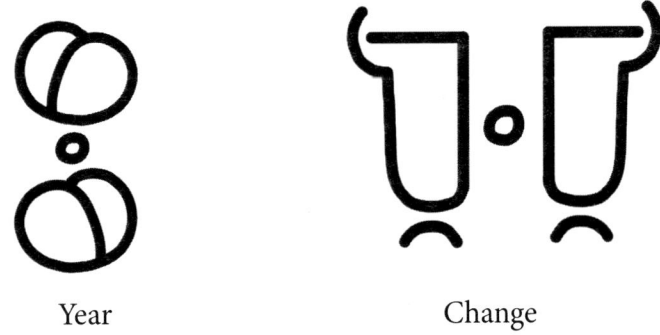

Year

Change

The *half steering mark* identifies when the hands turn opposite of each other on the sides, much like holding a steering wheel. The vertical line sets the "boundaries" of the up/down motion.

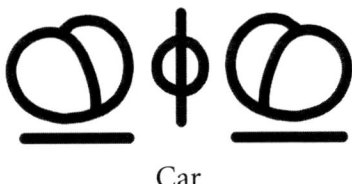

Car

Rarely, the half steering mark is written horizontally when the hands turn opposite of each other at the top/bottom.

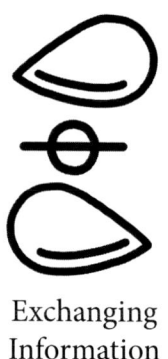

Exchanging Information

Our handshapes now have motion in neutral space. In the next chapter we'll explore signs that depend on spatial positioning in relation to the body.

Exercises:

Add movement marks to the digits and complete the words:

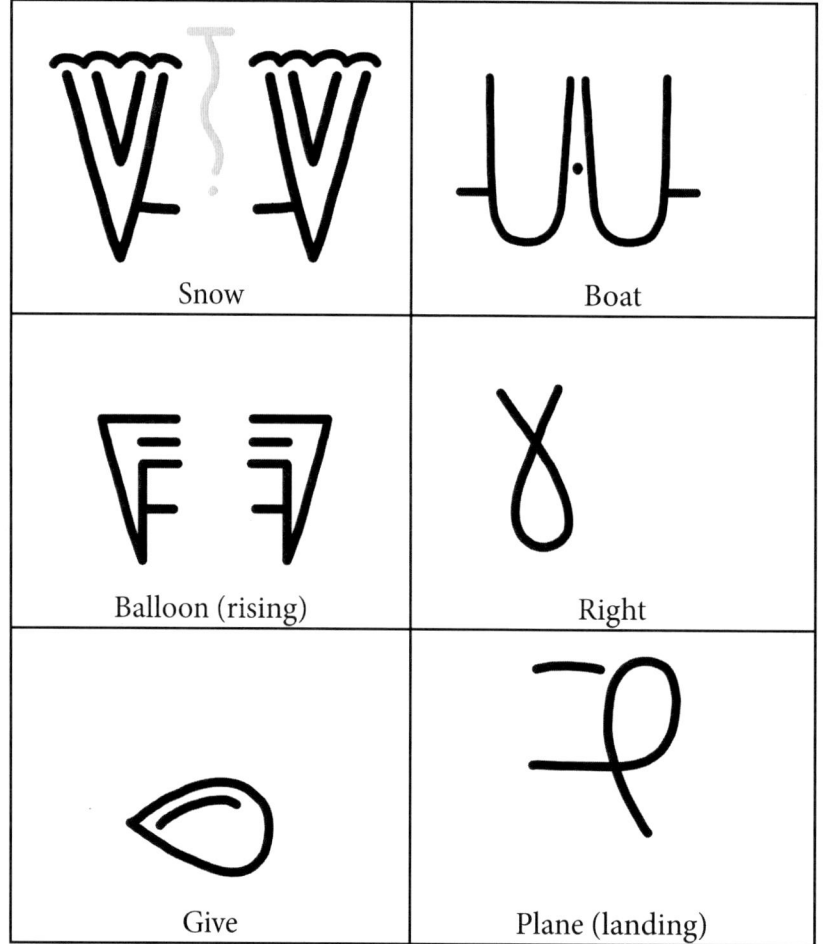

Snow	Boat
Balloon (rising)	Right
Give	Plane (landing)

Add a steering mark to the following digits and complete the words:

International	Socialize
Car	Wrap
Bike	Which

How to Write American Sign Language

Practice:

Chapter Four: Locatives

Spatial positioning in written ASL has two components: neutral space and locative space.

To review, *neutral space* is the area immediately in front of the body. Words expressed in that area are not "attached" to body position. They can be signed low or high and still be understood.

This is not so with *locative space*, because the meaning of the signed word depends on the proximity of the sign to the body. In written ASL, *locative marks,* or *locatives*, are used to show the part of the body that the sign is connected to. Those marks are also crucial for establishing palm orientation.

Locative marks have two viewpoints, the frontal and profile views.

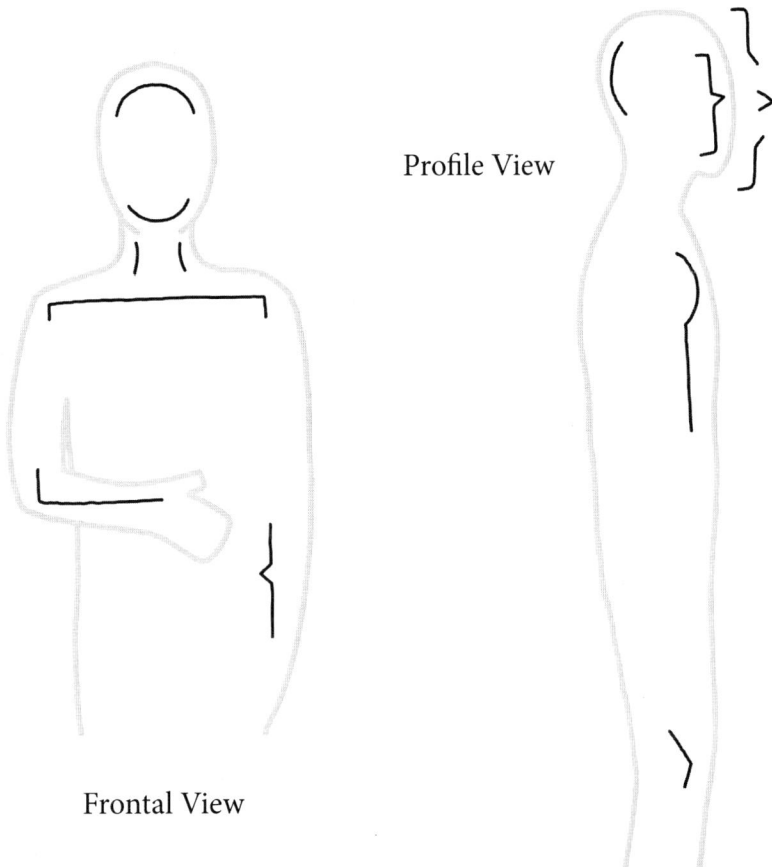

Profile View

Frontal View

Those two viewpoints are important, to identify whether a sign crosses the body (frontal) or moves outward from the body (profile).

How to Write American Sign Language

Frontal View

The locative marks of the *frontal view* are as follows:

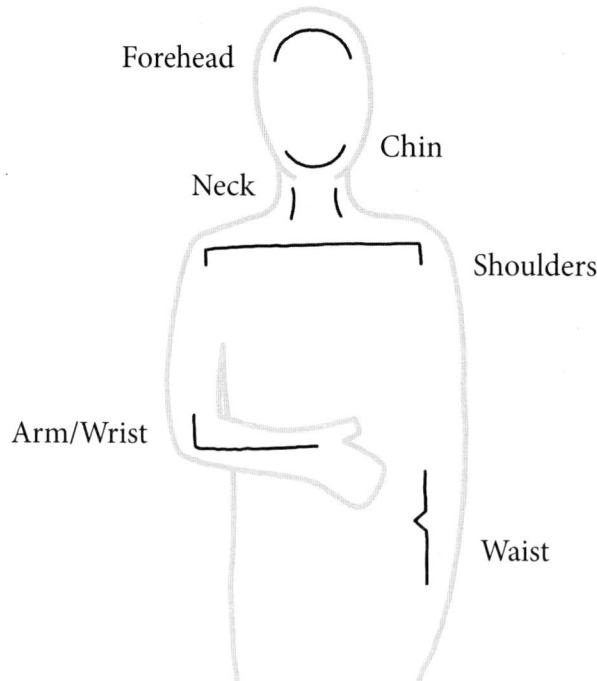

Motion lines and endpoints for this viewpoint are similar to the rules for neutral space, except that vertical marks are not needed.

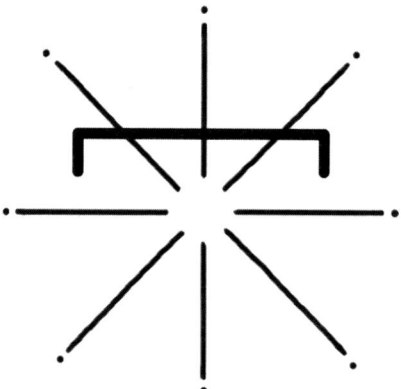

The digits are written on the same side as they are on your person. The following examples are written from the perspective of a right-handed signer.

Wonder   Dry   Please

Profile View

If a sign moves outward from the body, then the *profile view* is necessary:

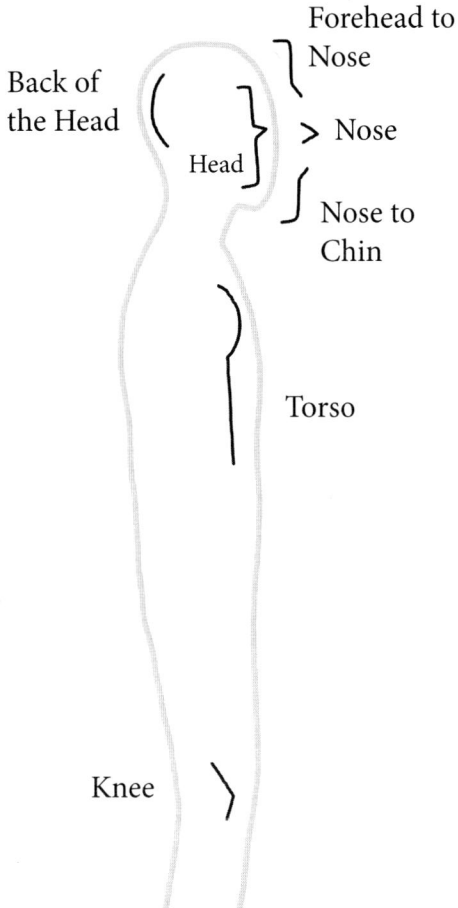

Motion lines for the profile view follow a different set of rules. Instead of following the signer's perspective, the marks are drawn from the perspective of the profile itself. This is also known as the third-person perspective in writing.

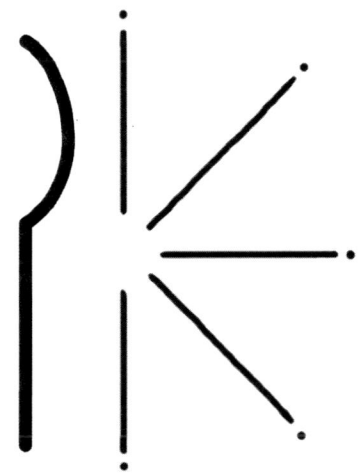

How to Write American Sign Language

The following words demonstrate the profile view, as written by a right-handed signer:

Hello　　　　　Kid　　　　　Tend

Sometimes when writing the digits, it is necessary to flip the locative mark to keep the correct digit for the dominant hand.

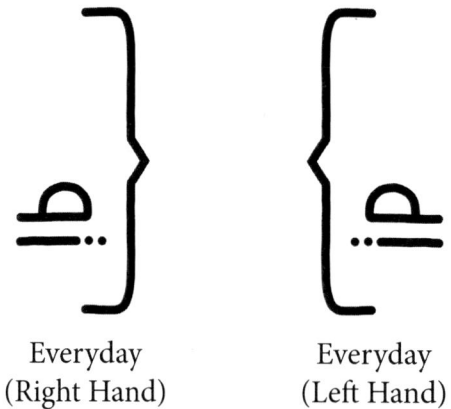

Everyday (Right Hand)　　　Everyday (Left Hand)

While digits by themselves can mean that the palms are either facing forward or facing downward, the usage of locative marks help distinguish the exact orientation. The following words are written by a right-handed signer:

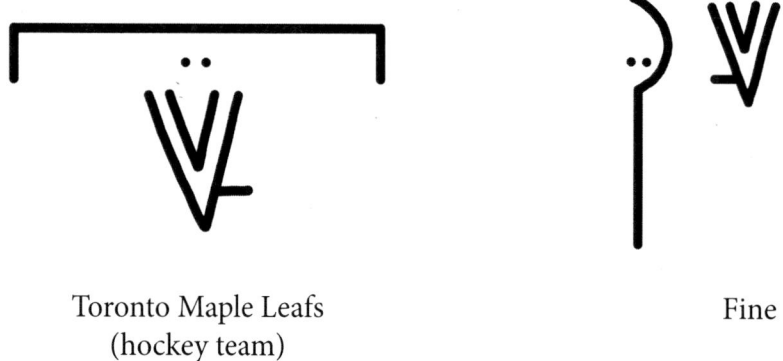

Toronto Maple Leafs (hockey team)　　　　　Fine

In writing the Toronto Maple Leafs' name sign, the shoulder locative mark firmly plants the hand flat on the chest. Just by changing the locative to the torso mark, a completely different word is created. This is how palm orientation can also be established by distinguishing locative marks.

In this chapter, we've studied the two spaces in which we write: neutral and locative. Next, we'll explore another important, nonmanual component.

Exercises:

Match the locative mark with the words below:

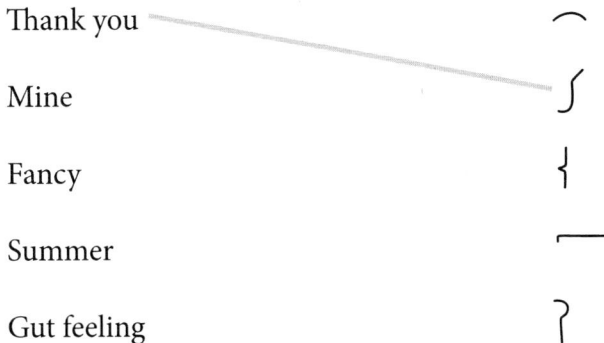

Write the full word.

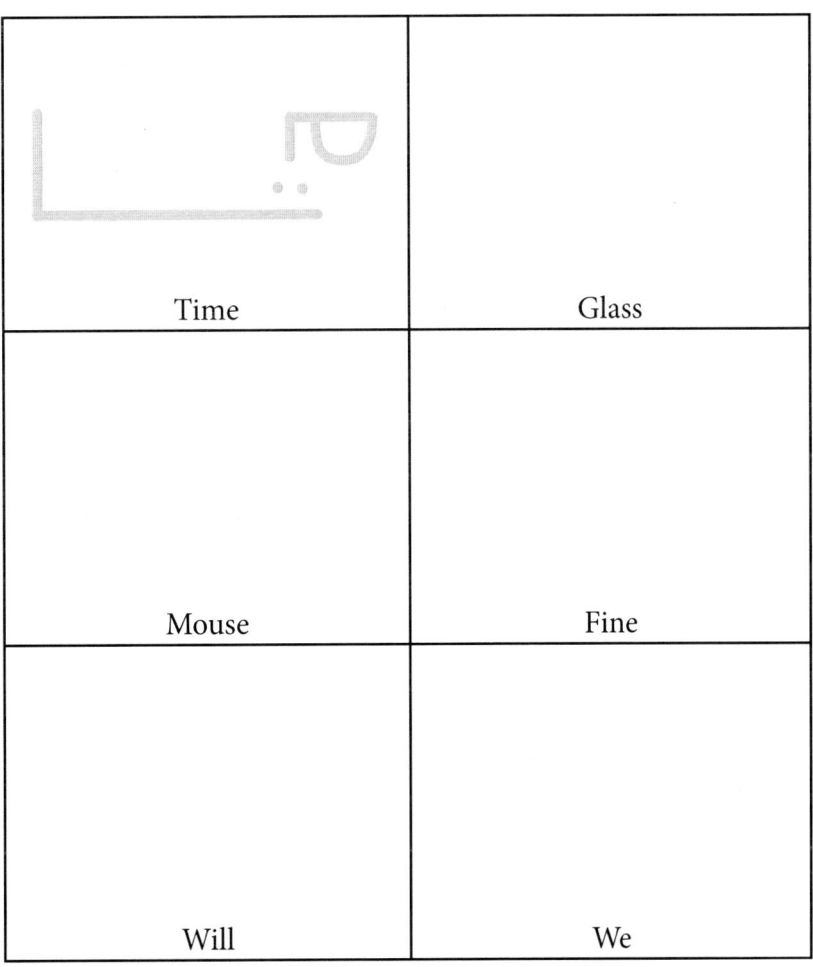

Practice:

Chapter Five: Extramanual Marks

We have covered four of the five components of expressive American Sign Language so far. The fifth, and final component is nonmanual signals, called *extramanual marks* in written ASL.

Nonmanual signals are the facial expressions and body movements that go alongside signs to add or establish distinct meaning. Those signals also have a major contribution to classifiers, special handshapes that show movement, location, and appearance. Including extramanual marks adds meaning to a digit and can also signify whether a digit is a classifier.

Extramanual marks have four categories: eyebrow marks, the nose mark, mouthing marks, and body motion lines.

Eyebrow Marks

The eyebrows are the largest portion of nonmanual signals. Their job is essential, especially when used as part of sentence structure. *Eyebrow marks* are either expressive or questioning.

Expressive marks are straightforward representations of facial expressions.

How to Write American Sign Language

Two of those expressive marks form the basis for the *questioning marks*. They are the raised eyebrows and knit eyebrows.

Raised Eyebrows   Knit Eyebrows

Raised eyebrows in expressive ASL either means that the signer is asking a question, or indicating the topic of the signed sentence. When writing a question, raised eyebrows bracket the sentence. Topicalization only requires the raised eyebrows to be immediately before the word.

Hello?   Walking is good.

Knit eyebrows are a hallmark of wh-questions. By changing the design of the eyebrows we get an individual mark for specific questions.

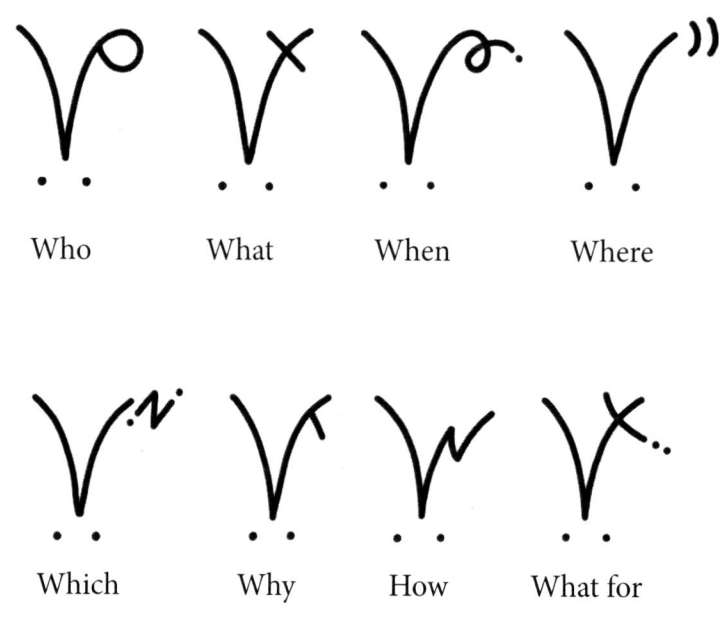

Who   What   When   Where

Which   Why   How   What for

For rhetorical questions, questions in which an answer is not expected from the reader, both questioning eyebrow marks may be combined.

John went to the store. Why? He needs food!

The Nose Mark

There is only one nose mark—the *crinkle*. It's used as a sign of agreement or disgust, depending on the context.

Nose Crinkle

Mouthing Marks

Mouth movements give weight to signs, expressing a specific meaning. They are also heavily used with classifiers. In writing, they are called *mouthing marks*.

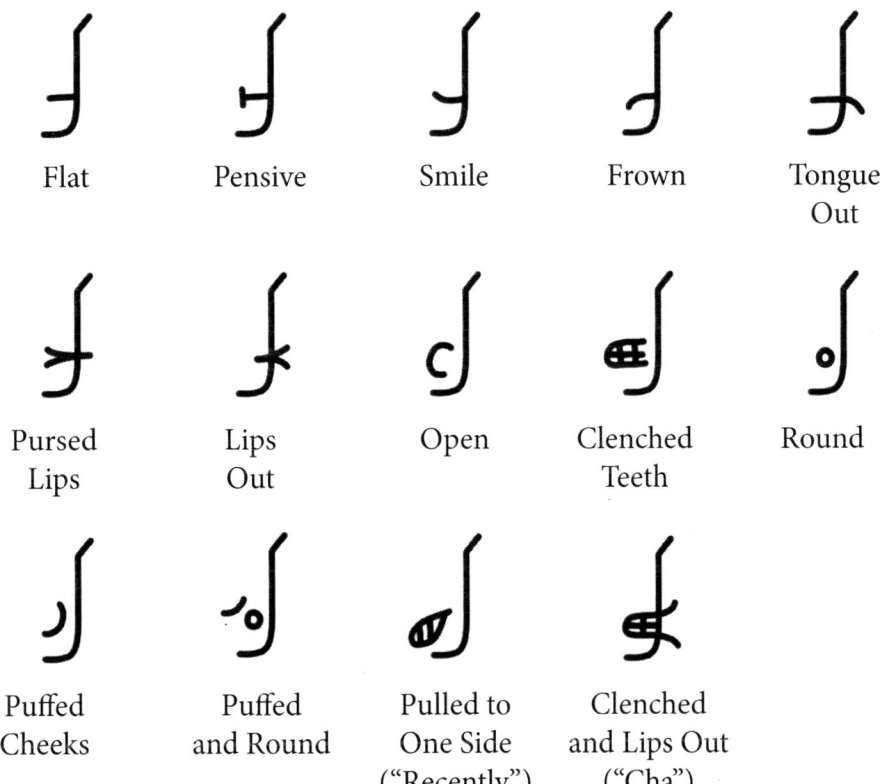

Flat   Pensive   Smile   Frown   Tongue Out

Pursed Lips   Lips Out   Open   Clenched Teeth   Round

Puffed Cheeks   Puffed and Round   Pulled to One Side ("Recently")   Clenched and Lips Out ("Cha")

The nose mark can be combined with mouthing marks, sometimes for dramatic effect.

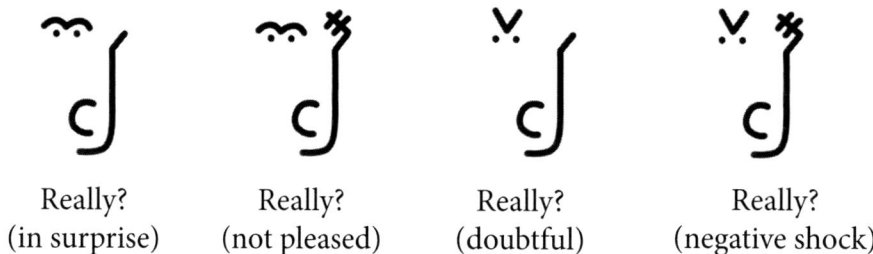

| Really? (in surprise) | Really? (not pleased) | Really? (doubtful) | Really? (negative shock) |

Body Motion

Once in a while, body parts move in a certain direction when signing. For example, the head may nod forward or the shoulders may move from side to side.

Head Nod · Shoulder Shift

The placement of extramanual marks takes some care and attention. In a straightforward representation, where the focus is on the expression, the mark takes up the space usually reserved for a word.

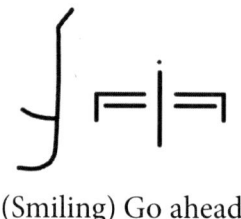

(Smiling) Go ahead.

However, when combined with words, the extramanual marks take up the upper left-hand space.

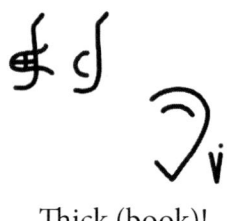

Thick (book)!

How to Write American Sign Language

Body shifts take up the upper right-hand space when they occur.

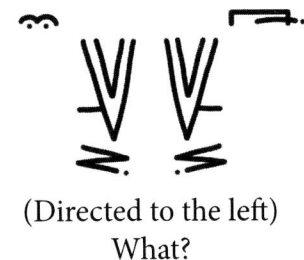

(Directed to the left)
What?

We've touched on all five main components of written ASL. In the next chapter we will explore the tools that tie those components together.

Exercises:

Match the extramanual mark with the word.

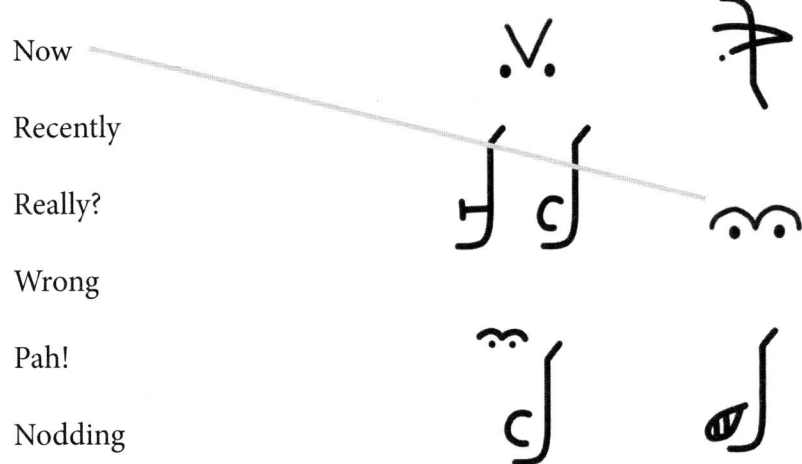

- Now
- Recently
- Really?
- Wrong
- Pah!
- Nodding

Write the correct extramanual mark for the following questions.

Who?	Where?	How?
Which?	What for?	When?

How to Write American Sign Language

Practice:

Chapter Six: Indicators

Much like English punctuation marks, a special class of marks helps modulate concepts and structure when composing a written manuscript. More marks may be added over time as written ASL evolves, but at present there are three parts: pronoun, grammar, and dropped indicators.

Pronoun Indicators

The basic concept of you and me is shown through the *index mark*. It resembles a pointing hand, with the index finger extended.

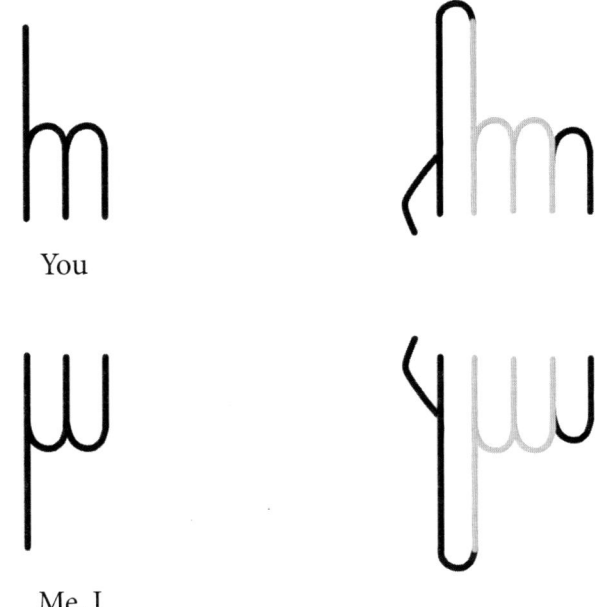

You

Me, I

When the subject is an "it," or a person/item/concept not within proximity, a contact point is added to the tip of the index mark.

It

How to Write American Sign Language

In rare circumstances, a *gender mark* appears before the index mark.

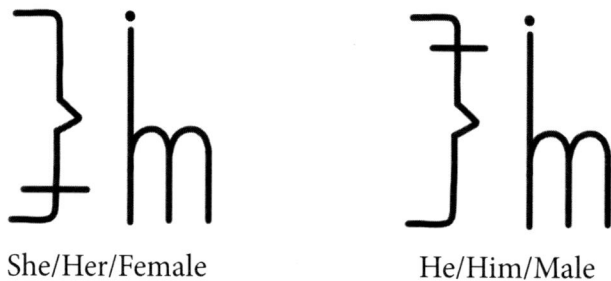

She/Her/Female   He/Him/Male

For a plural "you," a motion line is added.

They, Them, Those

One of the hallmarks of ASL is the *pronoun shift* (also known as constructed dialogue). When two or more people are engaged in conversation, the shoulders and eye gaze move to clarify the "sides" in a dialogue. We write this by using two indicators.

Shift 1   Shift 2

The *person mark* stands for one human being, and provides a counter for more than one person.

One Person   Two People   Three+ People

The mark can be written in place of "people," but most commonly comes after a verb to define an individual's job.

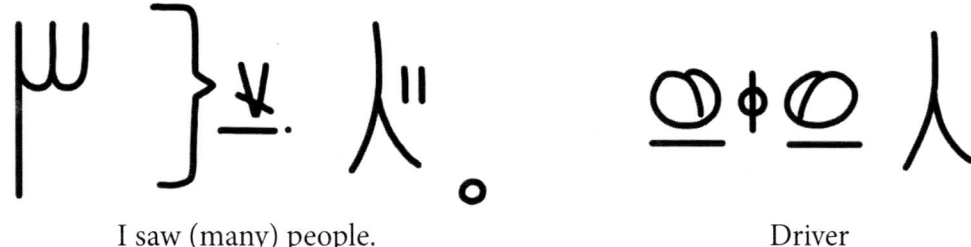

I saw (many) people.　　　　　　　Driver

If the pronoun is an animal, the *animal mark* is written instead of the person mark. It also keeps count.

One Animal　　Two Animals　　Three+ Animals

Grammar Indicators

When the signer momentarily stops at the end of a sequence of signs, a *pause* is written in order to separate concepts or phrases.

Pause

It functions much like the period in written English.

Hello Bob.

How to Write American Sign Language

When a signer stutters at the beginning or end of a sentence, several pauses are placed in sequence. This is called the *delay pause*.

Delay Pause

Sometimes a pause lasts for longer than one beat. A modified motion line is written, creating an *extended pause*.

Extended Pause

Dropped Indicators

Dropped indicators are unique in that they're halfway between a complete word and the symbolism of the other indicators. All the marks are kept, but the digits are completely dropped. This group has two sections: time indicators and action indicators.

Time indicators signify the times of the day. They show the position of the forearms and the wrists.

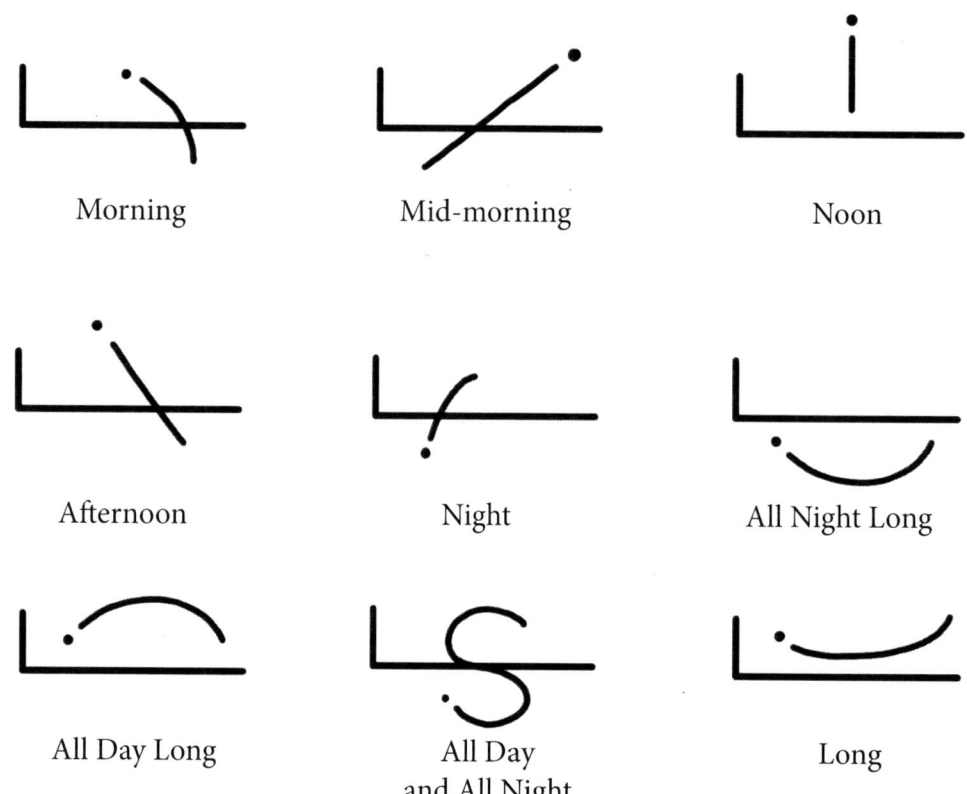

Action indicators are words whose motions are clear enough to warrant dropping the digits. "Come" and "go" are the only two established examples so far. This category is not as large as time indicators but may expand as written ASL evolves.

Come   Go

Now we have all the tools necessary to connect written words into sentences. The next step is bringing everything together with a dive into composition.

Exercises:

Match the indicator with the word:

Come

Noon

Pause

Two Animals

They

Afternoon

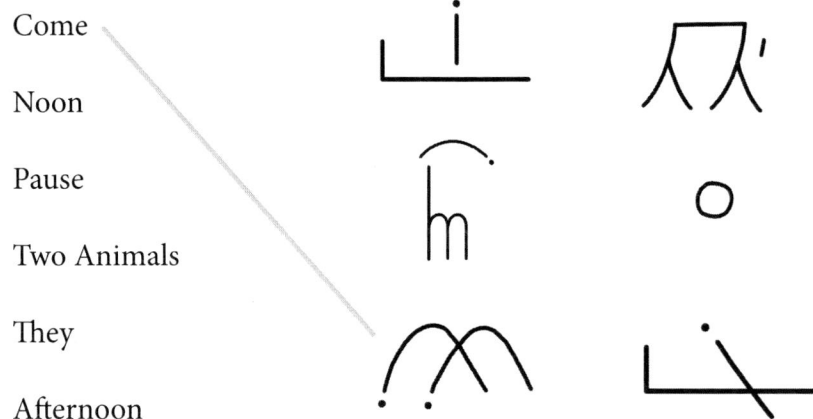

Write the correct indicators that would be used if the following phrases were translated:

He's here.	What a long wait!	I studied all night long.
Will you go?	Good morning!	There are many people inside.

How to Write American Sign Language

Practice:

Chapter Seven: Composition

We've covered all the components of written ASL, and now it's time to make the jump from bits and pieces to complete, cohesive writing. In order to write in ASL clearly, we need to look at the process of expressing a written thought.

The three levels of composition are: word, sentence, and paragraph. Each stage grows and builds on the one before, with the final stage being an article, or even a book.

Writing Words

To start writing a word, first we explore the sign itself and how it might fit on the page. Here are three "blueprints," one for neutral space and the other two for frontal and profile locative spaces.

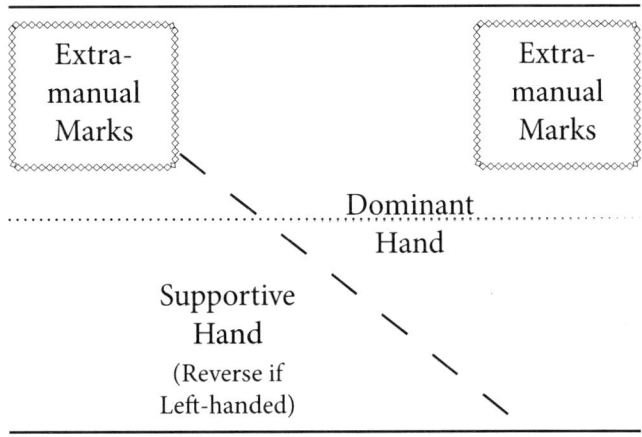

Neutral Space Blueprint

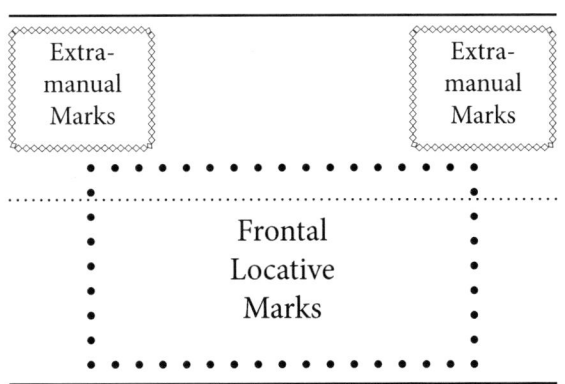

Frontal Locative Space Blueprint

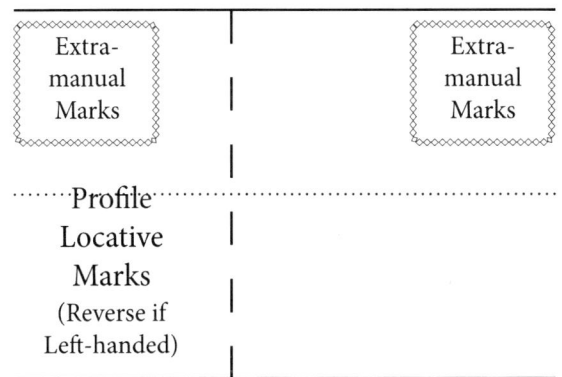

Profile Locative Space Blueprint

How to Write American Sign Language

The process is similar to the sequence in which you read through previous chapters. Let's take the ASL sign "support" for example. While a photo is provided for reference, we will be writing as if we were signing it ourselves. This first-person perspective is constant, even if you are transcribing live or from video.

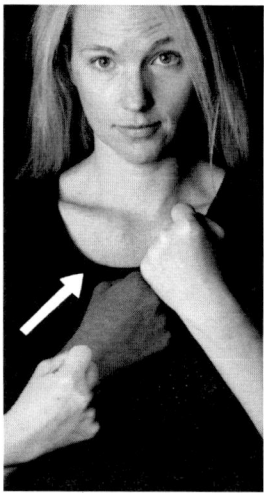

First we look at the handshapes and then match digits to them.

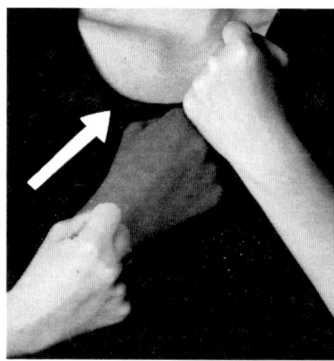  

After the digits are found, we determine whether the space used for "support" is neutral or locative.

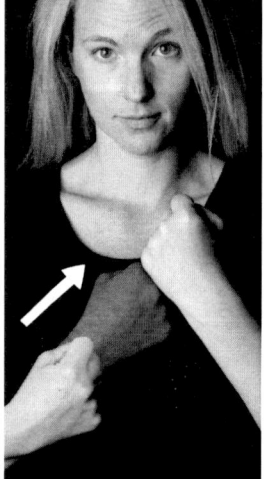 

How to Write American Sign Language

While the sign can be written using locative space, the extra mark doesn't contribute to understanding the word. Therefore, neutral space is best.

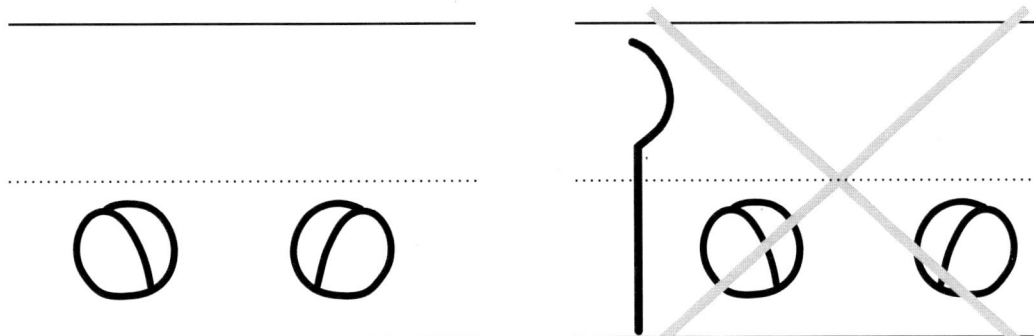

Now that we have determined the digit and space, we make the sign move by adding motion lines. When deciding what endpoint is used, the speed of the sign is gauged. If neutral, then regular endpoints are fine. An emphasized sign gets the firmpoint.

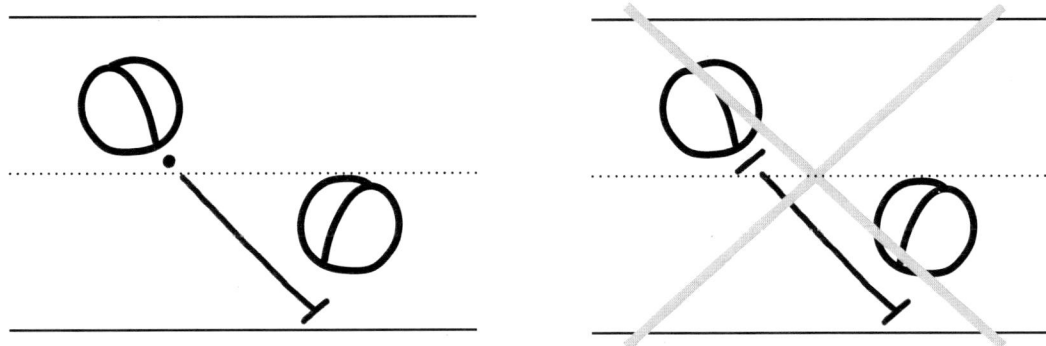

In this case, the signer did not emphasize the sign, so endpoints are left in. Next we look at the expression. If it's neutral, an extramanual mark is not necessary. Here in the example, the signer's eyebrows are raised to signify topicalization.

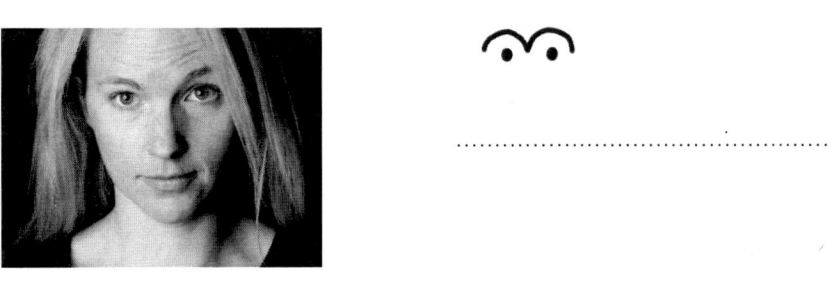

How to Write American Sign Language

All of the components are in place, and we now have the final word.

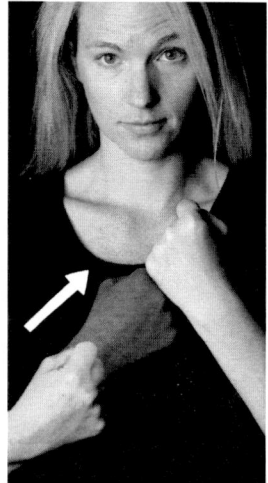
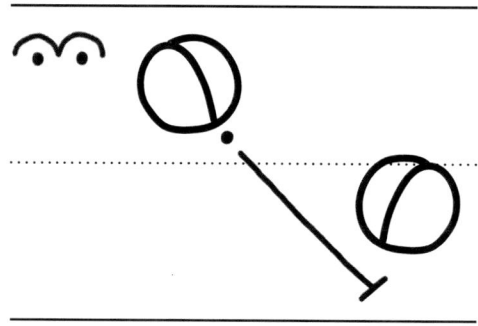

Let's go back and explore the process of writing a word using locative space. Our example is the ASL sign "thank you."

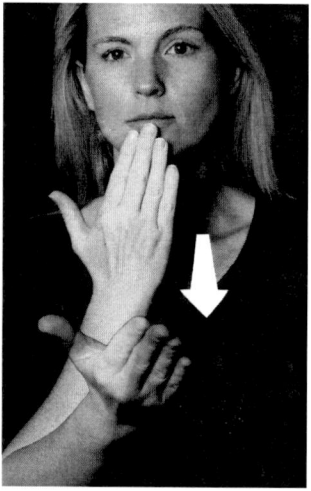

As previously done, we first determine the digits. The left hand is not included because it has no contribution to this sign.

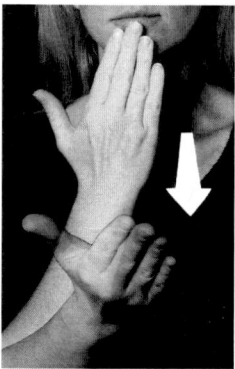
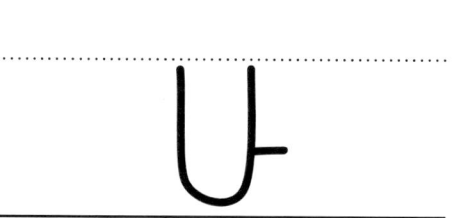

How to Write American Sign Language

We have already determined that locative space is best for this word, as it is incomprehensible without a fixed location. The head locative mark is the default choice, but the nose-to-chin mark is just as effective for this sign.

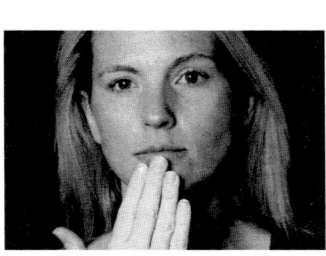 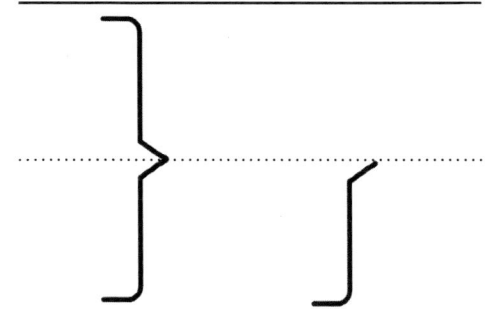

Adding a motion line wraps up the word.

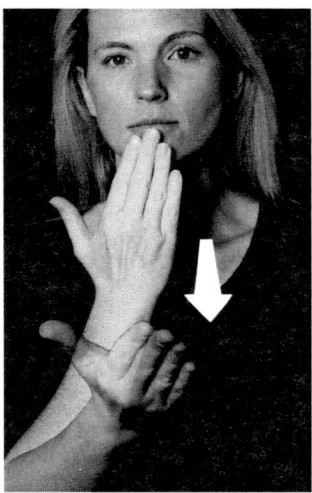 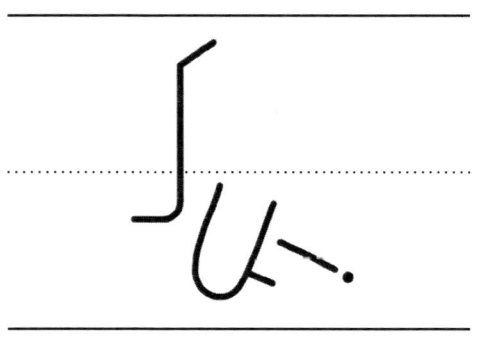

Some heavily-used words may even drop components for economy, but it's preferable to use the "formal" written form first until the writing community reaches consensus.

For example, the early version of the word "pah!" was fairly complex. Compare it with the current form.

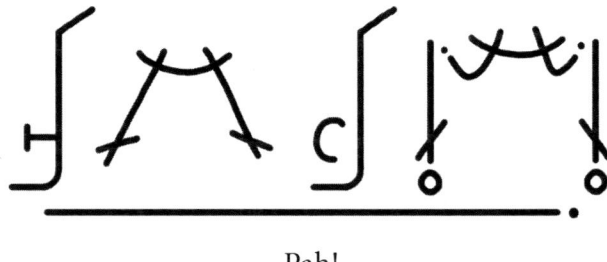 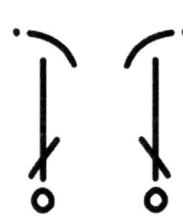

Pah!
(Formal/Original Form)

Pah!
(Current Form)

How to Write American Sign Language

The latter form of "pah!" is more efficient than the true form. It's much like how the English word "gasoline" condensed to the vernacular "gas." The usage also depends on the intended audience. Someone who is writing an academic essay would most likely use the initial form of "pah!," while a comic strip's punchline would use the condensed form.

One tricky situation is with writing double-handed signs in locative space. The three choices you have in this situation are: Write both left/right hand digits from the locative perspective, merge the digits (if they touch each other), and drop the non-dominant digit. Writing both digits is most effective when the spatial location of the hands are different. For example, the word "goal."

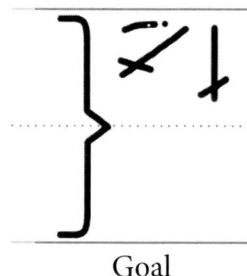

Goal

Merging the digits works best if the handshapes touch each other. "Pray" is one good demonstration. The proper term for digits that merge are *combined digits*. It can also happen in neutral space, as in the word "plumber."

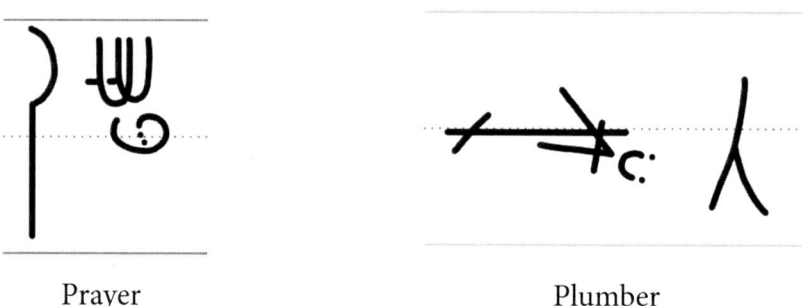

Prayer   Plumber

It's safest to drop the non-dominant digit if the sign can still be understood without it. Take "Thanksgiving" for an example.

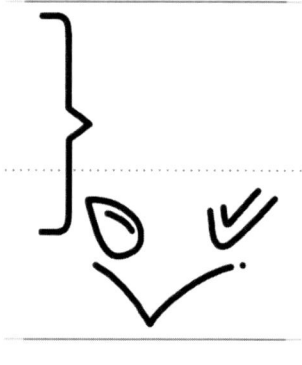

Thanksgiving

One point in regards to neutral/locative space is the establishing of a first-person and third-person view. Neutral space is the natural space one takes in signing, and writing in this perspective puts the reader in your mind's eye. Locative space is also the third-person view, as if there were a film camera rolling as you write. There are many possibilities with creative usage of neutral and locative space.

Writing Sentences

A few things to keep in mind: Questioning expressive marks bring attention to the topic of the sentence and at the beginning of a sentence, it tips off the reader that a question might be asked. There are some situations in which you might want to drop the indicator and write the actual sign. For example, if your character in a novel is from Iowa, you'd probably choose to write out "where" instead of "what" to match the local dialect.

Remember that you don't have the privilege of conversational feedback in writing as you would have talking with people in person. Take time to think from the perspective of the reader. If you use a regional sign and your audience is not native to your region, then you might want to write the word first, then spell it out afterwards. For example, the Minnesotan word for "outside":

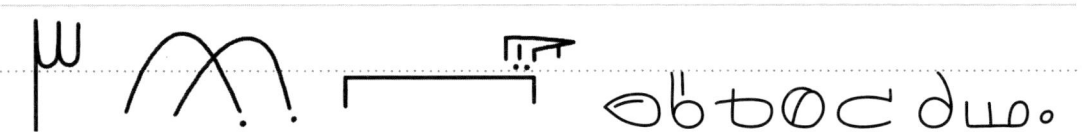

I am going outside.

It's not necessary to overexplain, but until the body of work in written ASL hits a critical mass it's better to be safe than sorry.

Pronoun shifts are done within the sentence. When the shifts are extended, such as in continued dialogue, then break it up into separate paragraphs.

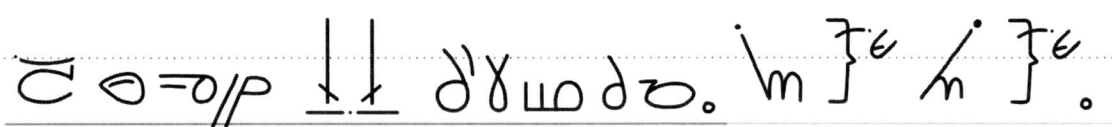

John met Freda. He said "Hello," and she said "Hello."

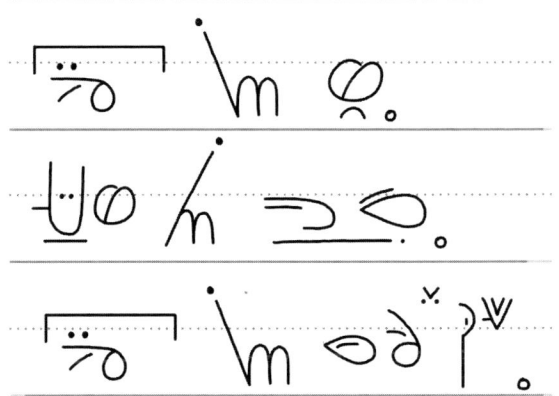

Paul said, "Yes."

Susan said, "No."

Paul said, "Ok, fine!"

How to Write American Sign Language

If a single shift occurs, then use the "it" pronoun indicator.

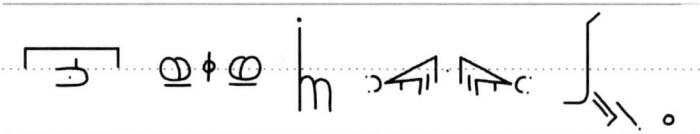

My car's engine runs well.

To practice clarity in writing, sign out what you want to say before you write it. Over time you'll get fast enough that you can simply visualize the word and write it on the page. Be patient as your skill progresses. Some ideas for practice: Grocery store lists/to-do lists, transcribing videos and plays.

Writing Everything

Keep in mind that written ASL is NOT a notational system. It's normal to try and document everything that goes on in a sign when you start. Once you see what parts are essential to understanding the core message, you'll be able to write accurately and avoid redundant marks and lines.

That's why it's important to recognize the difference between a performance in ASL and the written counterpart. If we transcribed Clayton Valli's classic *Dandelions* poem, for example, only the most important aspects are retained. The reader has room to imagine the style and appearance of the signer. A small sample follows:

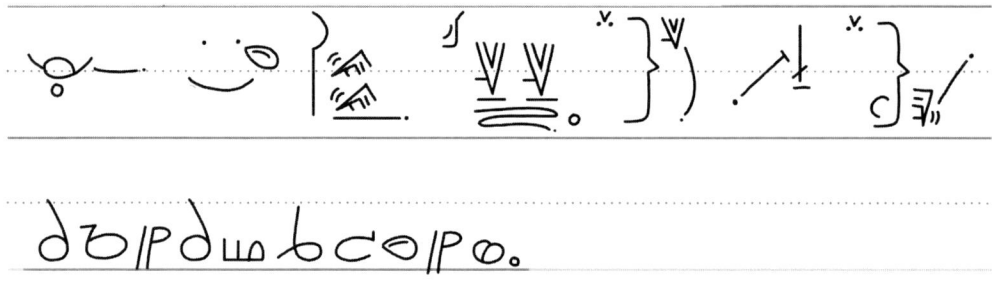

Generally the composition rules of English and other written languages apply when composing paragraphs and overall subject of materials. An exception occurs where you would normally pause in conversation for the other signer to interject. In this situation, you could start a new paragraph, and obliquely address what the other signer might respond, or the topic can be modified slightly.

In closing, the key thing with written ASL is to remember you already know the expressive language. There's a learning curve in becoming a fluent writer, but it's not impossible. Things become easier with more practice, so always look for opportunities to write.

Best wishes on your journey to fluency!

Practice:

Resources

As of this edition, we do not have a complete font for written ASL, but technology has offered us many alternatives. To start, you can write on paper and scan it in as a image to attach in email or post on your favorite social network. Alternatively, use a digital tablet and your favorite drawing program. A Wacom tablet and Adobe Photoshop are two good choices.

A faster method is to use a drawing app on the iPad/iPod and other personal devices. A few options are:

Bamboo (wacom.com)
Paper (fiftythree.com/paper)
Handwriting (cocoabox.com)

All of those apps have buttons that allow you to write and share via email. They may have Facebook and Twitter share buttons as well.

For further support, visit ASLwrite.com for more resources, email groups, and forums. The Si5s organization (si5s.org) also offers workshops and training in written ASL.

Open Digits | Expanded ASL Digibet | Left Hand

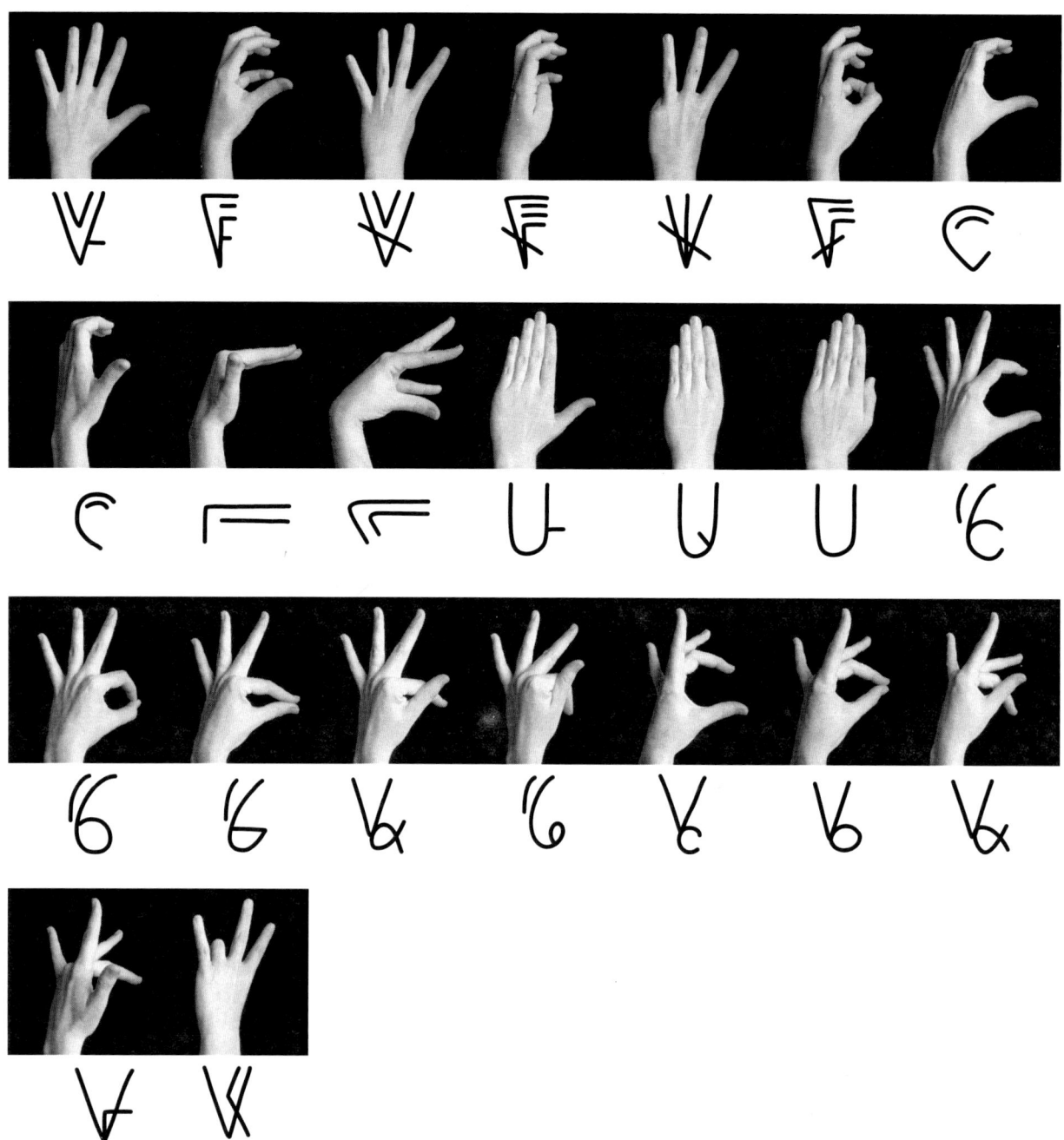

Right Hand | Expanded ASL Digibet | Open Digits

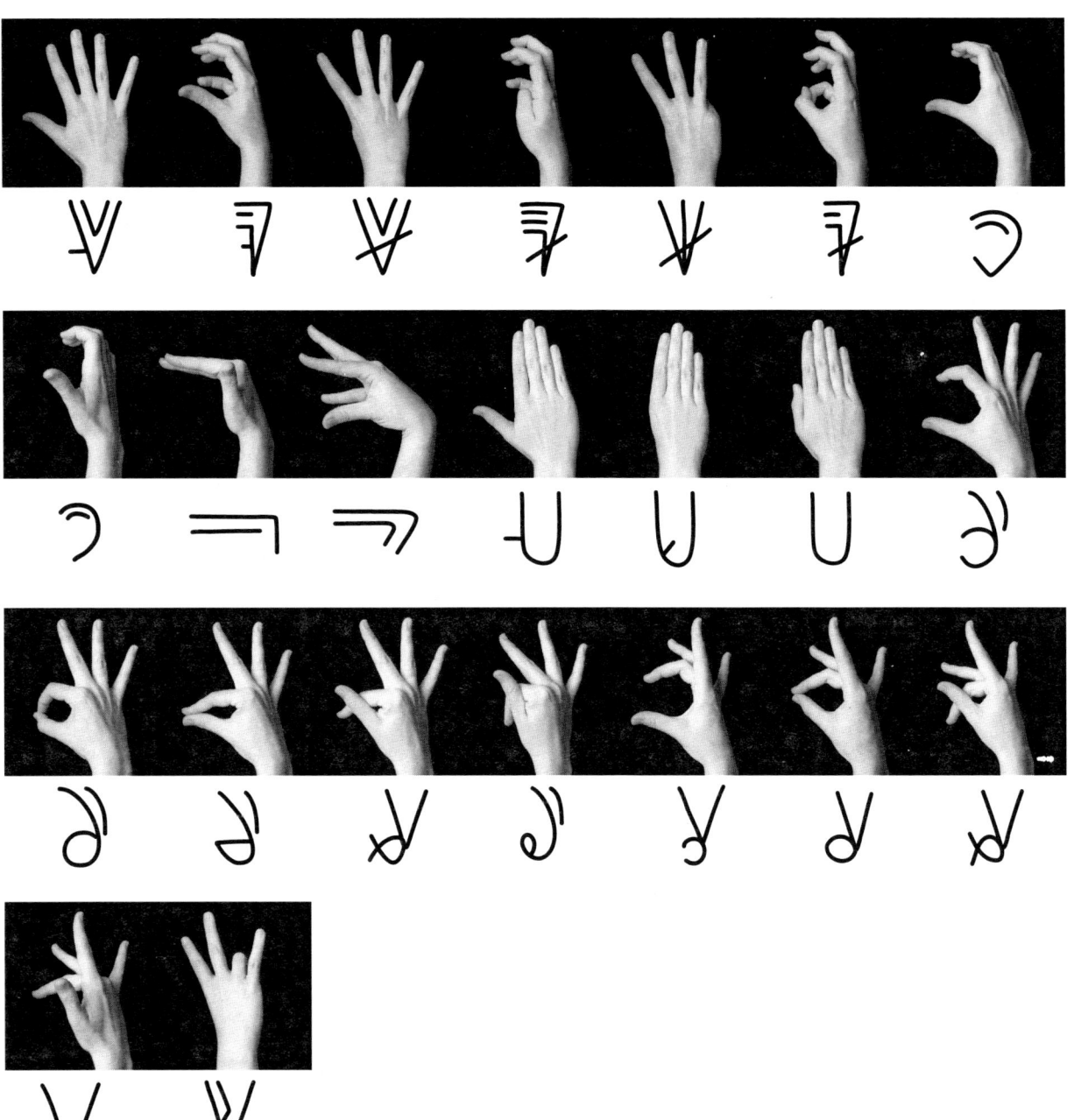

How to Write American Sign Language

⬤ Closed Digits | Expanded ASL Digibet | Left Hand

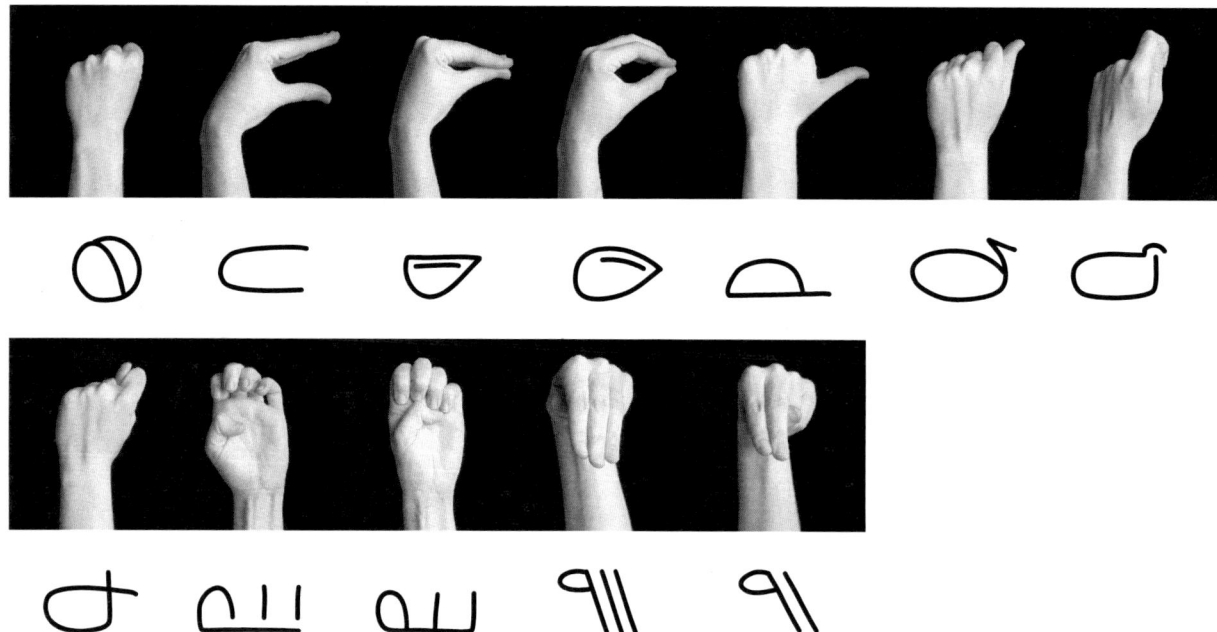

Right Hand | Expanded ASL Digibet | Closed Digits

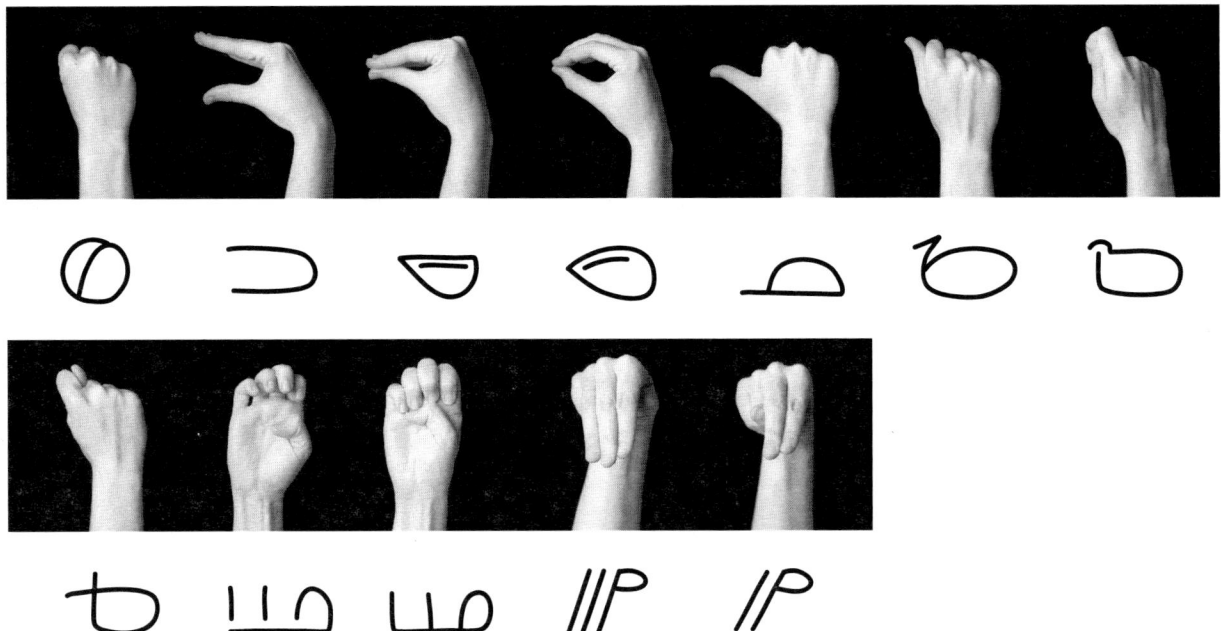

Mixed Digits | Expanded ASL Digibet | Left Hand

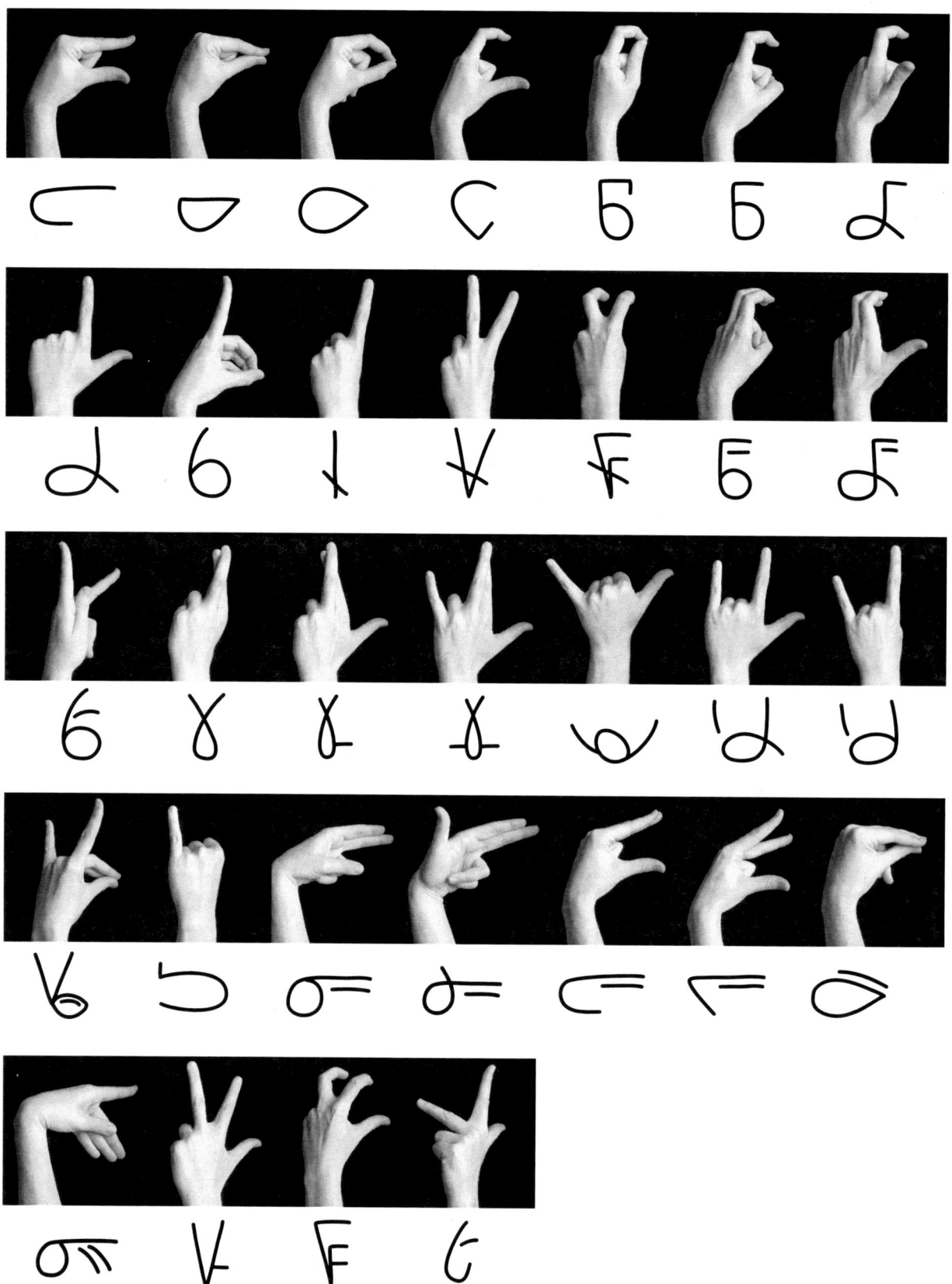

Right Hand | Expanded ASL Digibet | Mixed Digits

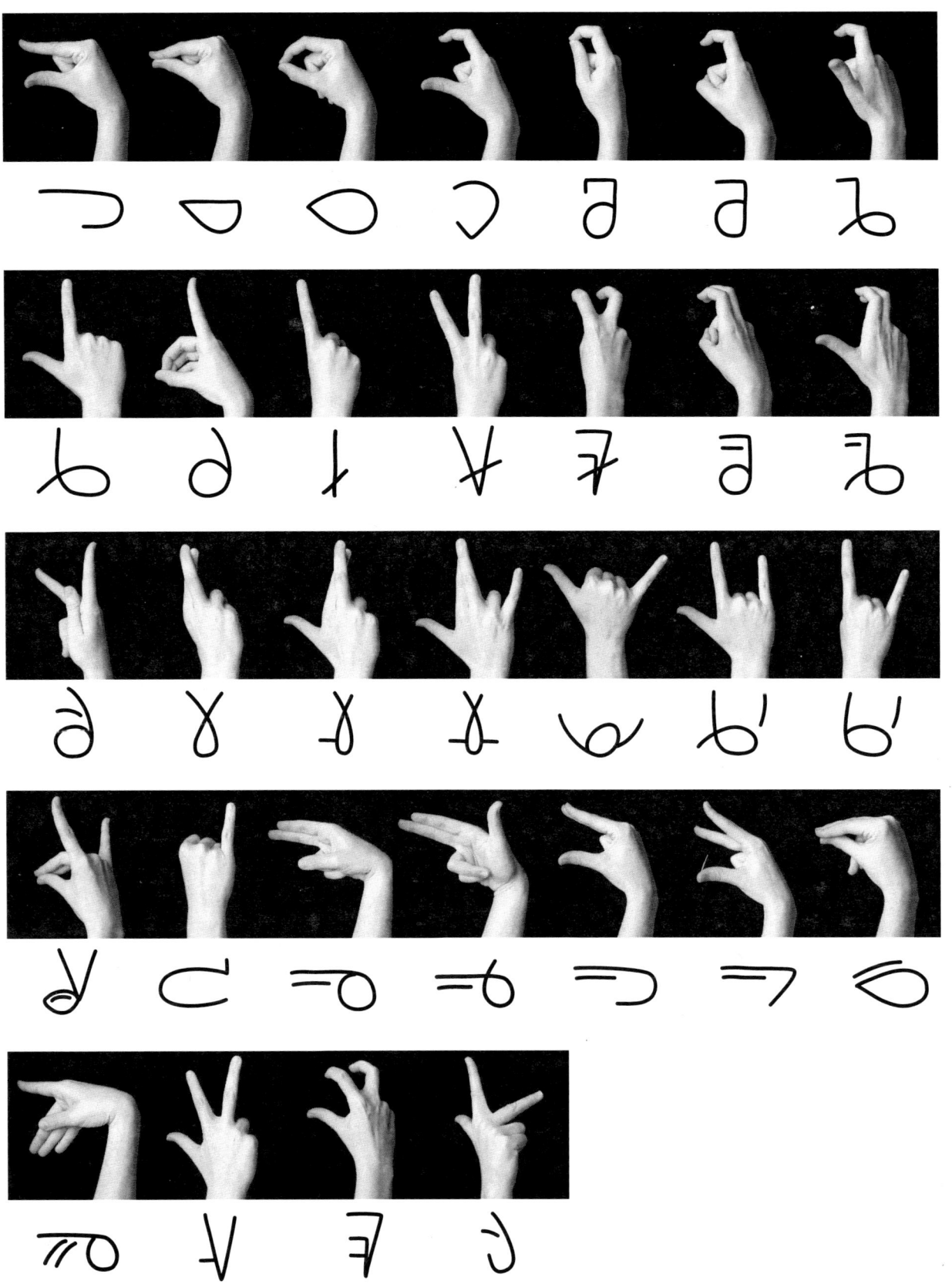

How to Write American Sign Language

Answer Key

Chapter One: The Digibet

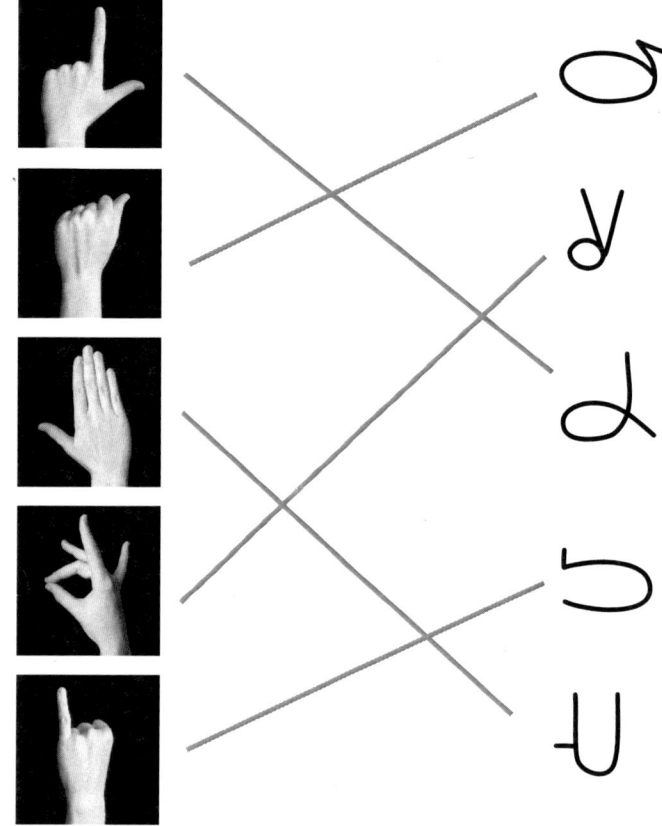

EDWARD (LEFT-HANDED)

ELIZA (RIGHT)

JEAN MASSIEU (RIGHT)

AGATHA HANSON (LEFT)

J. SCHUYLER LONG (LEFT)

Chapter Two: Diacritics

Apple	⌒	⊙ (circled)	~~~	⟩⟩	—
Snow	⌒	○	~~~ (circled)	⟩⟩	—
Must	⌒ (circled)	○	~~~	⟩⟩	—
Dog	⌒	○	~~~	⟩⟩ (circled)	—
Machine	⌒ (circled)	○	~~~	⟩⟩	—

Basketball	Tomorrow	Wheels
Wait	Red	Snow

Chapter Three: Movement Marks

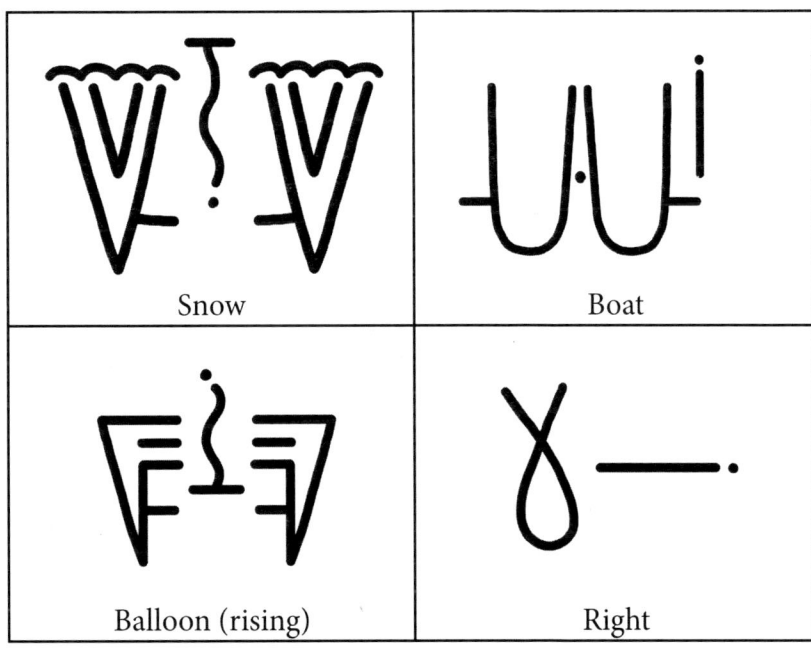

Snow	Boat
Balloon (rising)	Right

How to Write American Sign Language

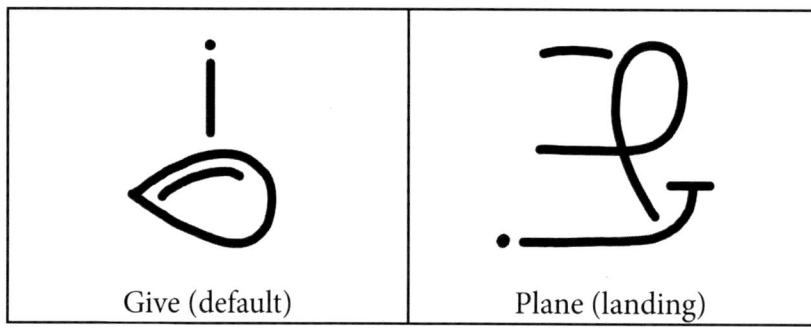
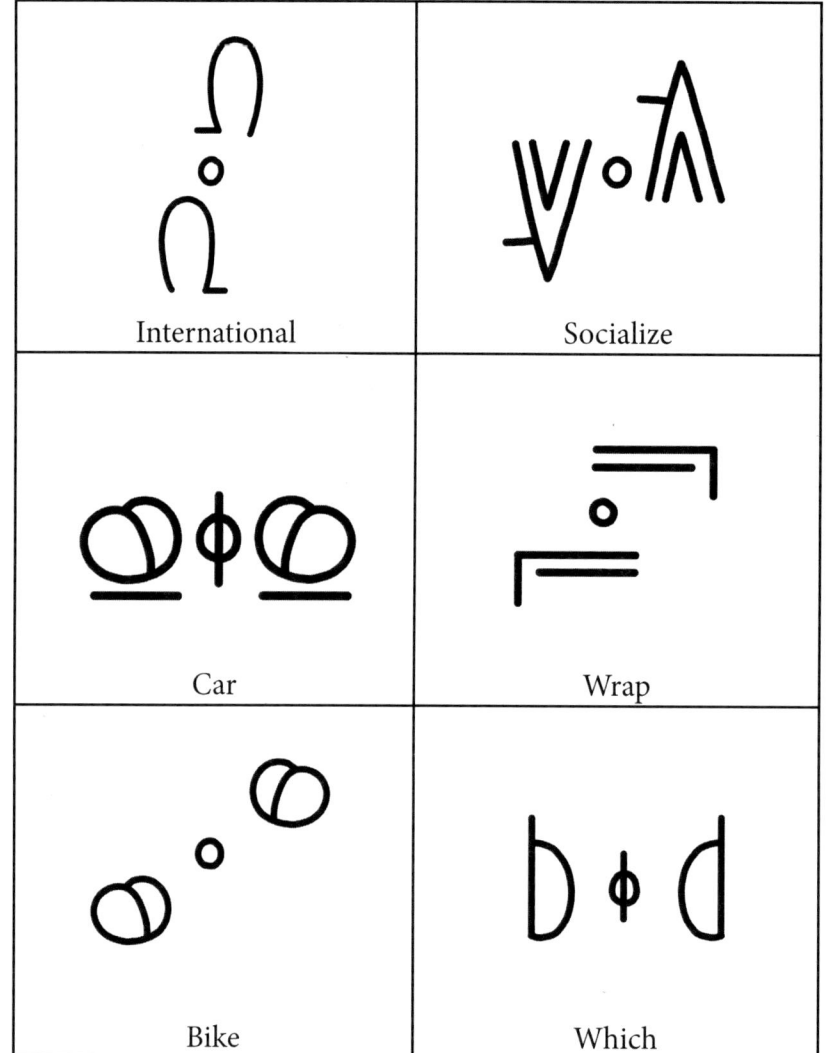

Chapter Four: Locatives

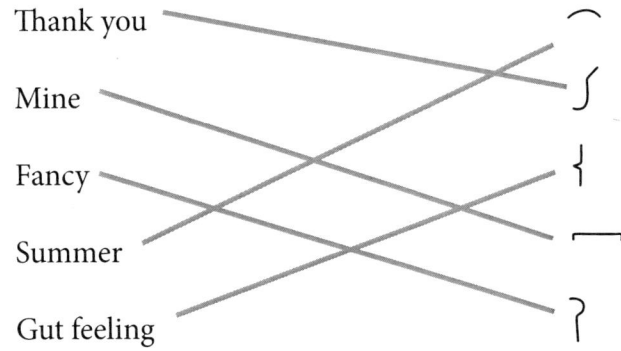

Chapter Five: Extramanual Marks

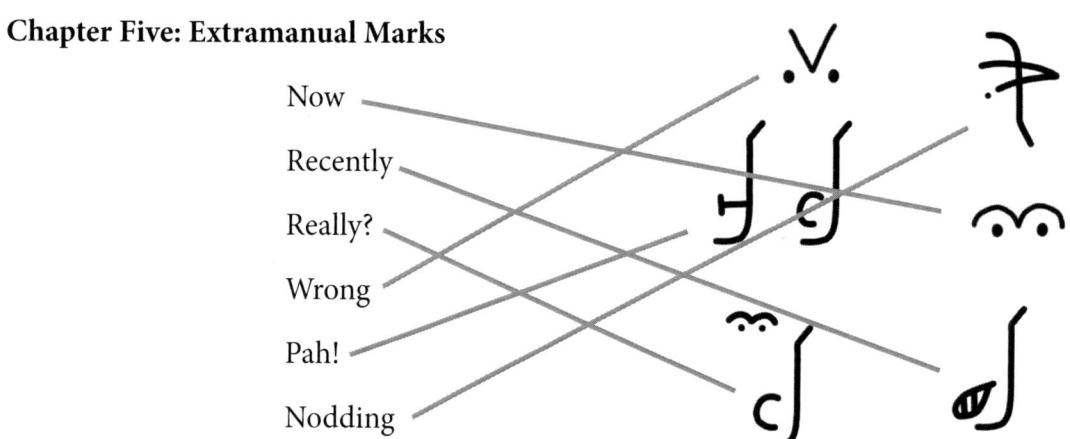

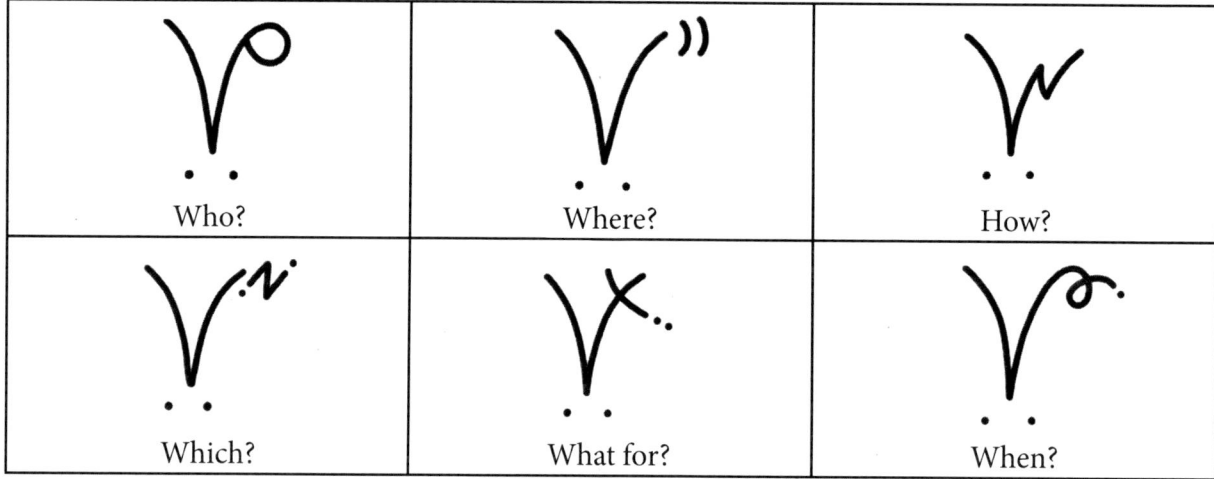		
Who?	Where?	How?
Which?	What for?	When?

Chapter Six: Indicators

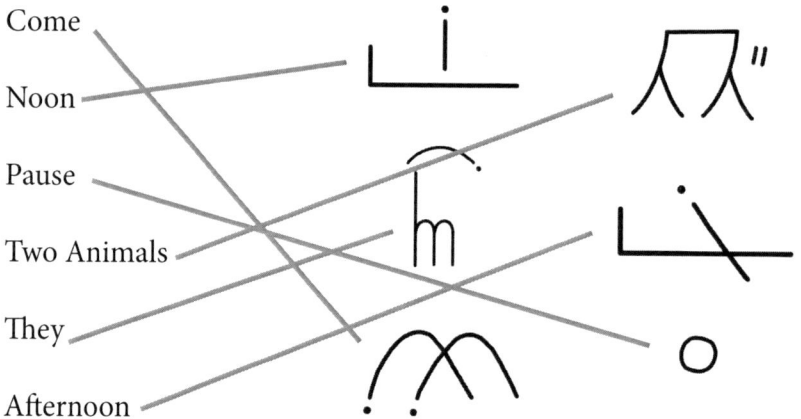

He's here.	What a long wait!	I studied all night long.
Will you go?	Good morning!	There are many people inside.

About the Author

Adrean Clark is a Deaf writer and illustrator. She has published several books, including *8 Ways to Be Deaf*, *The Census Taker and Other Deaf Humor*, and the *Survival ASL* series. Adrean frequently translates her comics into written ASL. All of her work can be found on adreanaline.com.

Printed in the United States of America.
Typeset in Minion Pro, Myriad Pro, LetterOMatic, and Si5s Energy.
To order more books, visit aslwrite.com or email order@aslwrite.com